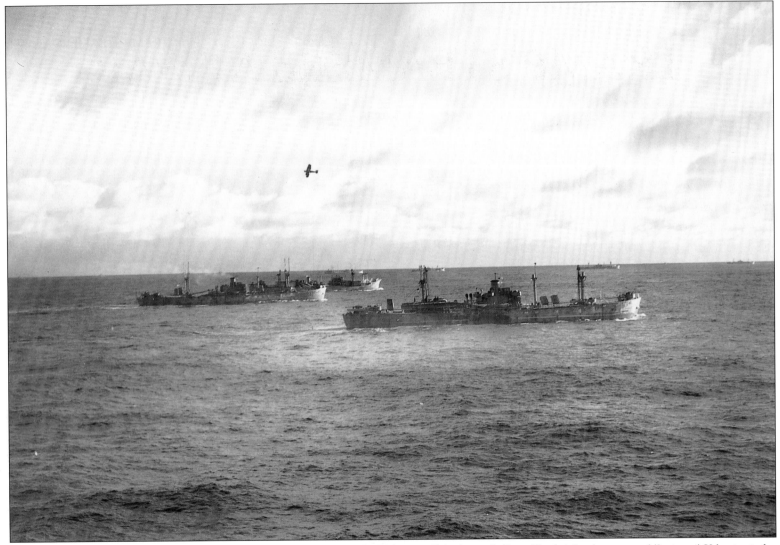

Photo taken from the escort aircraft carrier HMS *Chaser*, showing one of the ship's Swordfish planes circling a North Atlantic convoy while on anti-U-boat patrol.

(Imperial War Museum)

TRAMP STEAMERS AT WAR

George Gunn

GOMER

First Impression—1999

ISBN 1 85902 634 6

Printed in Wales at
Gomer Press, Llandysul, Ceredigion

CONTENTS

The largest convoy in history of British Navy and Merchant Navy ships on its way to the Invasion of French North Africa in November 1942. It consisted of more than 500 Naval and Merchant Navy ships and was heavily protected by RAF Coastal Command, RAF Bomber Command and US Army Air Force.

(Photo taken from an aircraft of RAF Coastal Command, Imperial War Museum)

Foreword

I thoroughly enjoyed reading Captain George Gunn's book *Tramp Steamers at War* prior to publication. The whole story of his apprenticeship reflects a remarkable effort of memory, and is a familiar story to so many of us who served our time at sea learning to be seamen.

In some respects my time on oil tankers wasn't quite so tough, not being away from UK ports on long arduous voyages, slowly tramping round the world under the most primitive conditions. Sailing on four of these steam vessels during wartime, George Gunn has given us hugely interesting and entertaining accounts of life on board a breed of ship which no longer exists and which played such a major part in the nation's survival.

Commodore Charles Colburn OBE

Commodore
Charles Colburn, OBE.

Two convoys passing port to port, taken from bow of HMS *Eglinton*.

Preface

For almost 100 years British registered ships sailed the oceans of the world unchallenged by other maritime nations. General cargo vessels, colliers, oil tankers, passenger liners and large numbers of coasters, ferries, dredgers and fishing vessels totalled more than 6000 at the outbreak of war in 1939. In 1999 there are about 200.

Over 90% of the ships sailing in North Atlantic convoys were tramps. *Tramp Steamers at War* is a personal narrative about four of these vessels in wartime and about the seamen who manned them.

Hogarth's Baron Line owned the largest UK fleet of tramp ships with a world-wide operation controlled from their offices at 120 St. Vincent Street, Glasgow. By September 1939, there were 39 Baron Line steamers; twenty of them were sunk during the war. The company additionally managed another 36 cargo vessels, all owned by the Ministry of War Transport. Twelve of these were also lost to enemy submarines and aircraft.

Hogarth's became shipowners in 1870 and between then and the start of World War One in 1914 they operated a total of 33 cargo vessels, 28 of which were lost at sea. It obviously didn't need a war for tramp owners to lose their ships. In peacetime, stranding, collision, fire and abandonment, and ships lost without trace for unexplained reasons, was a price that often had to be paid to run a world-wide tramp steamer business. During 1914 to 1918 another 18 were sunk, although the loss of life was considerably less than it was to be in 1939 to 1945. Much more humanity was shown towards crews of ships attacked by the Germans in 1914 than by the Nazis in the 1940s and their Japanese allies.

One unexpected merciful act in 1942 which saved the lives of many seamen took place during a submarine Wolf Pack attack on convoy SL125 bound for the UK from Freetown. Several of the 37 ships in the convoy had been torpedoed and were either sunk or sinking. During one sustained attack s/s *Baron Elgin* turned round to stop and rescue survivors from other ships. A surfaced U-boat, seeing what the master of the *Elgin* was trying to do, withheld his fire, circled the ship and allowed him to take all the men on board and sail for Madeira where they were safely landed. *Baron Elgin* lasted out the war and was scrapped in 1960.

The other 'Baron Boat' in the same convoy wasn't quite so fortunate. *Baron Vernon* was torpedoed and sunk by U-604, one of the eight units of the Wolf Pack. Some time before that she had sunk after colliding with another vessel in the Firth of Clyde and on that occasion had been salvaged and refitted for further service at sea.

This book tells a personal story of wartime experiences sailing as a Deck Apprentice, 3rd Mate and 2nd Mate on four of the ships which fortuitously survived. I feel fortunate to be able to write about it so many years afterwards and hope it will provide some answers to some of the many questions about life at sea on board British tramps in a time of war.

George Gunn

Introduction

By 1941 there were few good reasons to go to sea in the Merchant Navy. One thousand British ships had already been sunk by enemy action. The Ministry of War Transport didn't divulge statistics, but it was known that huge losses and casualties were being inflicted every day, mainly in the North Atlantic.

Sitting alone in the train compartment from Glasgow to Greenock to join my first ship, these were the last of my thoughts. I had started school at Dowanhill Primary in 1928 just as the Great Depression was beginning to bite. It must have been evident by then that politicians' promises after the Great War 'to build a land fit for heroes to live in' wasn't happening.

My father was killed by a bus in 1926, after fighting in France throughout the war with the Gordon Highlanders. My stepfather was back at sea on merchant ships. The two previous vessels he served on were sunk by U-Boats. Understandably, my mother didn't want me to go to sea as well.

As the engine puffed and jolted down the line, I mentally checked out the bits of gear carefully packed in the old leather suitcase wobbling precariously in the string luggage rack opposite. My last job as a salesman in the sports outfitters had been a godsend. The manager knew I was only working there until accepted by some shipping company as a deck cadet or apprentice on one of their vessels. He kindly gave me a generous discount on most of the new items in the case. Payment was by weekly deductions from my wage of twenty-one shillings and sixpence, which was balanced by an appropriate increase. The shop didn't stock sea-boots so an old pair of mother's high-heeled wellingtons had to do.

Four years' apprenticeship, a second mate's certificate, another three years' sea-time for first mate, three more for master and seeing the world at someone else's expense; a piece of cake, I thought. I had not understood until then that the owners of my first ship had lost almost half their large fleet of cargo vessels to enemy action, mainly in the North Atlantic.

The indentures were signed and in my pocket was a letter addressed to 'The Master'. The previous nine months were spent writing to shipowners for a job. During that time I regularly attended night classes on navigation and seamanship at Glasgow Royal Technical College, and felt ready in all respects for sea.

Deck apprentices on pre-war and wartime tramp ships contributed considerably to their economic operation. They were the only members of the crew on term contracts in excess of the usual Voyage Articles of Agreement. When a ship reached its final port of discharge in the UK and the crew were signed off, the apprentices kept things going until the new deck crew signed on. This was as near as possible to departure time for the next trip. Home leave for apprentices was scarce.

Indenture remuneration was £5 for the first year, £10 for the second, £15 for the third, and £20 for the fourth. One pound a month good conduct bonus was available but not guaranteed. Should the four year Indenture period expire during a voyage the apprentice agreed to serve in the ship until arrival at a port in the United Kingdom at a rate of £3 a month. This included an allowance for washing.

An apprentice was discouraged from breaking into the £50 indenture money. It was expected to be used towards the cost of obtaining a second mate's certificate. The War Risk Bonus and good conduct money, if any, provided the pay-off at the end of a voyage after deductions for subs., cigarettes and tobacco, and a small (voluntary!) contribution to the Royal National Lifeboat Institution. The mystery remains why the monthly war-risk value of a cadet, deck boy or galley boy was £3, when other crew members received much more.

Tied to a company for four years, an apprentice was available for 24 hours a day, 365 days a year, with no maximum working hours or claim to shore leave or vacation periods. According to the Indentures, this allowed sufficient time for them to be taught navigation, seamanship and the business of a seaman. All reference to a Ship's Officer are deleted and initialled in the margin by a parent or guardian.

CHAPTER 1   Starting out from Glasgow

Before the war Glasgow's population was one million. The Clyde was custodian of the world's largest ship building industry. It was a terminal port for Atlantic liners and the headquarters of many major shipping companies. Glasgow was a great seaport and produced marine engineers who manned thousands of vessels sailing under every national registration. Standing on the top grating of a ship's engineroom anywhere and shouting, 'Jock, are you down there?' would guarantee at least one positive reply.

During the 1920s and early 1930s Glasgow was a typical example of the privations and degradation unemployment brought to so many highly-populated areas of the British Isles. Thousands of men from shipyards and other once vibrant industries hung around street corners. It was a scene of hopelessness, but to a youngster being brought up there it was a normal way of life. Cinemas, or picture houses as they were known, provided some relief from the conditions. In 1930 the Standard in Partick was still showing silent films. For a weekday or Saturday matinée it was a penny a seat on the wooden benches in the front stalls. Any not occupied when the programme started were sold to those first in the queue in the lane at the side for a clean refundable lemonade bottle.

Two hundred yards along Dumbarton Road, the Western Cinema had begun to show talkies. The front seats in the stalls for *Ben Hur* were threepence. Ex-servicemen who had lost limbs in the war sat on the low walls of the Kelvingrave Park, and elsewhere outside the city centre, selling boxes of matches for a penny. Five Woodbine in an open top paper packet cost tuppence, although small local shops would sell one cigarette and a couple of Vulcan or Swan Vestas matches for a ha'penny.

A couple of weeks in Glasgow Western Infirmary in 1931, for what was then a serious operation, had a profound effect on my education. I was sent to Ullapool in the Highlands of Scotland to recuperate. It was common to hear Gaelic there and the grandparents I stayed with spoke it all the time. It ensured that I did so as well. Ullapool once more became 100% Gaelic-speaking.

Life in this remote area was sustained by manual work. Two weeks in the Western Infirmary had prepared me for some of that. Probably due to the Depression, mutual aid between patients was expected and accepted. At a point in recovery from an operation we helped to sweep the long wooden floors of the wards, take cups of tea to those less fortunate, and bring them bedpans where necessary. That was sufficient incentive to get well enough to get out of there as soon as possible.

Ullapool has often been described as the prettiest village in Scotland and few could argue with that. Apart from fishing boats, the only access was via Inverness to the railhead at Garve, then a further thirty miles by solid-tyred stagecoach on a very rough single track road with passing places. Strangers going there had to have good reasons for doing so.

Our Market Street cottage had no drainage, electricity, gas or running water. The pump was at the end of the street. One of my jobs was filling enamel buckets with drinking water and galvanised ones for other domestic purposes. Water from rain butts was used for washing clothes and satisfying the needs of two cows and other animals. Oil lamps provided light, and were little used in summer but continually in winter. Then for long periods I went to school and returned in the dark. Being snowed up for as much as a week at a time, when the mail coach couldn't get through, was a frequent occurrence. There were no newspapers, letters or other contact with the outside world. Long summer days atoned for that.

By June 1938 there was some job stability for school leavers. The Depression years were over. An engine fitter earned three pounds a week and youngsters starting work, up to ten shillings. The Fifty Shilling Tailors was being undercut by the Thirty Shilling Tailors which had opened a shop in the centre of Glasgow's busiest thoroughfare, Argyle Street. Made-to-measure suits would never be so cheap. again

Attendance at the 'Buroo School' was required of boys leaving school who had no prospects of employment after two weeks. This was to ensure that ability matched ambition. The first question asked 'What do you want to be? – revealed engineers, bus drivers and salesman.

I opted for electrical engineer. This was approved. The boy standing next to me said labourer. This was also approved.

Russell Moreland's Sports Emporium under the Central Station bridge took me on as apprentice salesman at nine shillings a week, less fourpence for insurance. The hours were eight to six, and nine o'clock on Saturday, with a half-day off on Tuesday. I learned how to sweep up, clean, dust, polish, wash shop windows and assess fairly accurately the contents of discarded paper bags and newspaper parcels left from the night before's activities under the bridge.

Glasgow Central Station Bridge on Argyle Street was nationally known as the Highland Man's Umbrella. It provided a well-covered promenading area where ex-pats from the Scottish Highlands and Islands met to chat in Gaelic and hope to meet friends or relatives from home. It was also used for more covert purposes.

Deliveries of heavy sporting goods, such as cast iron punchball bases to outlying districts of the city using Glasgow Corporation Transport, were regular features of this apprenticeship. The tupenny fare included the driver's help to lift the heavy objects into the front of the tramcar beside him and get them off and onto the pavement at the nearest stop to our destination.

I always turned up for work dressed for sales in my blue serge suit, white shirt and Hyndland School tie, but the opportunity to sell never came. The highlight of that career was walking up Union Street carrying two well-packaged square boxes and wondering what passers-by would think if they knew the contents. Benny Lynch, Glasgow's World Flyweight Champion, was defending his title at Shawfield Stadium the following night against the American, Jackie Jurich, and I was taking the gloves up to the promoter's office. This fight was the main talking point in the city, and I felt important for the first time in my life.

After six weeks I was made redundant. I thought Russell Moreland must have been going through really hard times to do it. Anyway, nine shillings a week less a three-shilling bus season ticket from home to work hardly covered the wear and tear on my blue serge suit.

I moved up Renfield Street to the kilt-cutting department of R. W. Forsyth, the Glasgow department store. Customers entering the shop were greeted by floor walkers dressed in tails and striped trousers. Mr.

Archibald, the kilt-cutter, worked upstairs in a small back room, similarly attired. I was his one assistant and carried the bundles of material for kilts, tartan jackets and trews across the lane at the rear of the shop to the girls working the sewing machines in an adjacent building. I learned all about Scottish tartans, and a lot about girl machinists.

Knowing I really wanted an apprenticeship of some kind, Mr. Archibald recommended me to Thomson, Son & Wright, a high class bespoke tailors on Bath Street. Among their wealthy clients was Glamis Castle, the former home of Lady Elizabeth Bowes-Lyon, our Queen. They also supplied a number of Glasgow shipowners, who ordered two or three business suits at a time, costing up to twenty pounds each.

The war started, and the prospect of sitting cross-legged on a wooden bench sewing up coats and jackets for the duration, or until called up for the forces, didn't appeal. With current rate of conscription, there were now plenty jobs available, so off I went along Sauchiehall Street to Lumley's Sports Shop as a salesman for seventeen and six a week.

Introduction to the wonderful game of golf, which I have pursued relentlessly for a lifetime, was during twice-weekly fire-watch vigils teamed with Lumley's resident professional Jack McMinn. He was a former tournament player attached to the famous North Berwick Golf Club. The problem of staying awake all night after a full day's work in the shop was solved with free golf lessons.

The war came nearer to home with heavy bombing raids on Clydebank and the shipyards. In Green's Playhouse, Oscar Rabin and his Romany Dance Band carried on playing. We kept on dancing, but not for long. The homeward trek back along Great Western Road towards the conflagration made Jimmy and me realise what an air raid really was.

My thoughts turned to the ship I was about to join in James Watt Dock. She was a typical flush-deck, deep-sea tramp steamer, built on the Clyde in 1935. Depending on weather conditions, the quality of the coal, the firemen and the engineers, her speed was between eight and ten knots on less than twenty tons of fuel a day. The owners described her as one of their large fleet of general cargo vessels, capable of carrying thousands of tons of all kinds of freight anywhere in the world.

Baron Renfrew. on which George Gunn served two years of his apprenticeship during the War.

My thoughts were interrupted by a shout from the platform: 'This is Port Glasgow. Next stop Greenock.'

The *Renfrew* was discharging a full cargo of sugar from the West Indies when Leo and I arrived together on the quayside. He was the other new apprentice and came well prepared for the career ahead, having just finished a full year's cadet course in Glasgow. His fraternal great grandfather had perpetuated the family name by running the blockade as master of a French sailing vessel during the American Civil War. Leo had worked with the sole aim of joining the Merchant Navy and was fitted out from truck to keel with everything necessary to carry on the Le Tessier marine tradition.

The First Mate, standing on deck at the top of the rope ladder, shouted down, 'You two, find a heaving line and get your stuff on board here.' Leo, knowing what the Mate was talking about, scrambled up the ladder and found one.

Apprentice seniority on tramp steamers was an important part of life. Leo, with his superior nautical knowledge, clinched that between us for the next couple of years by being first on board the ship.

Bill, the senior apprentice, was in the cabin when we got there. 'Now's the time to bag a bunk,' he said. 'There are only three bunks and a settee, and they're putting another apprentice on board this trip. Someone will have to sleep on the settee. Anyhow, the way they work

15

George Gunn,
the apprentice.

more expensive for the owners or shippers What the hell! it's wartime and the Government is paying. This crowd is so damned mean they can't get away from their old pre-war penny-pinching practices. You'll learn soon enough about these things. We'd better get on deck and see what he wants. The new crew hasn't been signed on yet. There are a few shore riggers helping here in port, but he can't get the work out of them like his own men when they're on articles. We fill in and do what is required. Old hands say apprentices are just cheap labour.'

Despite his formidable appearance, the Mate seemed to treat the apprentices with more consideration than expected. For most of the stay in Greenock he was the only deck officer on board and relied on us to pull our weight in every direction. Although the jobs were usually heavy and dirty, Leo and I relished the chance to tackle shipboard work we had only read about in *Nicholl's Seamanship & Nautical Knowledge*. Bill considered it a learning process, and having done it all before took a more advisory role.

Bill had been on the ship longer than anyone else. The last trip was uneventful, but the previous June in Convoy OG51 bound for Huelva in Spain they were attacked by U-boats and aircraft. A FW200 Condor strafed and dive-bombed the *Renfrew* and she was abandoned with an unexploded bomb impaled in the tank top in number three cargo hold. All the crew with the exception of the cook were safely taken off in the lifeboats. He continued to fire the ship's only armament, a Lewis Gun mounted at the stern of the vessel, and was killed.

The survivors were taken on board one of the escort vessels, a Royal Navy corvette, and spent eleven days in wild North Atlantic weather before arriving back in the Firth of Clyde to find their own ship lying there comfortably at anchor. It had been salvaged.

A couple of nights ashore in Greenock was enough to break in the new uniform. Leo's was sufficiently worn from the Cadet Course to dispel any suggestion of being a first-tripper. Mine required a gentle application of Cherry Blossom boot polish to tone down the giveaway lustre of the cap badge and little bits of gold braid. The uniform jacket and trousers had been bought very cheaply from an outfitters on Paisley Road West. He had generously contributed the cap and Merchant Navy officer's badge as part of his War Effort.

us on this ship, we won't often all be turned in at the same time. We'll work the hot-bed policy. You jump into the bunk vacated by the person relieving you on watch. It's OK in the winter in the Western Ocean but bloody uncomfortable in the Red Sea and Persian Gulf.' Leo said, 'This settee looks less than five feet long and I'm six feet.' I thought of my meagre five foot six and lack of seniority. 'Anyway,' said Bill, 'it depends on how long the other guy's been at sea and what he's like.' Bill's revelations of Barahona, La Romano and San Pedro de Macoris, where the sugar cargo was loaded, were abruptly interrupted by a voice booming out, 'On deck you lot, immediately.' This brought us back to the reality of Greenock Docks.

'What will we be doing? asked Leo. 'Don't worry, he'll soon tell you, and you'd better get these uniforms off. They won't be needed for a while.' Bill reckoned we would either be down the holds or oiling the winches. 'That's usual in port when the ship is discharging with it's own derricks. It's easier in places where there are dockside cranes, but it's

I. 1.

ORDINARY APPRENTICE'S INDENTURE (SCOTLAND).

It is contracted, agreed, and ended between¹ *H. Hogarth & Sons, Shipowners, 120, St Vincent Street, Glasgow C.2* on the one part, and² *George Smith Gunn* born the *8th* day of *June* 1923, son of⁴ *Roderick Gunn (Wine Merchant) (Deceased)* a native of *Glasgow* in the county of *Lanarkshire* and now residing at *48, Ripon Drive, Kelvinside, Glasgow* with the special advice and consent of⁴ *Daniel McCulloch Christina Gunn (Mother)* testified by his subscribing these presents on the other part, in manner following; that is to say, the said² *George Smith Gunn* with advice and consent foresaid, hereby binds himself Apprentice unto the said¹ *H. Hogarth & Sons* his Heirs and Assignees, for the term of *4 (four)* years from the date hereof; and the said Apprentice, with consent foresaid, hereby binds and obliges himself that during such time he will faithfully serve his said Master, his Heirs and Assignees, and obey his and their lawful commands, and keep his and their secrets, and will, when required, give to him and them true accounts of his or their goods and money which may be committed to the charge, or come into the hands, of him the said Apprentice; and that the said Apprentice will not, during the said term, do any damage to his said Master, his Heirs or Assignees, nor will he consent to any such damage being done by others, but will, if possible, prevent the same, and give warning thereof; and will not embezzle or waste the Goods of his Master, his Heirs or Assignees, nor give or lend the same to others without his or their license; nor absent himself from his or their service without leave; nor frequent Taverns or Alehouses, unless upon his or their business; nor play at Unlawful Games; IN CONSIDERATION WHEREOF, the said¹ *H. Hogarth & Sons* hereby binds and obliges himself, and his foresaids, during the said term, to use all proper means to teach the said Apprentice or cause him to be taught navigation and seamanship and the business of a seaman ~~and of a ship's officer~~ *and in the event of the said apprentice being unable to fulfil the terms of this indenture through ill health, it will be at the option of H. Hogarth & Sons to cancel this indenture,* and the Master also agrees to provide the said Apprentice with sufficient Meat, Drink, Lodging, Washing, Medicine, and Medical and Surgical Assistance, except in so far as such Medicine and Assistance is provided under the National Health Insurance Acts, and pay to the said Apprentice the sum of £ *50 (fifty)* in manner following: (that is to say,) *for the first year five pounds, for the second year ten pounds, for the third year fifteen pounds and for the fourth and last year twenty pounds. Should this indenture expire during a voyage the apprentice agrees to serve in his ship until arrival at a port in United Kingdom at the rate of three pounds per month. These amounts are to include allowance for washing* the said Apprentice providing for himself all ~~sea-bedding~~ wearing apparel, and necessaries (except such as are hereinbefore specially agreed to be provided by the said Master): AND IT IS HEREBY AGREED, that if, at any time during the said term, the said Master, his Heirs and Assignees, provide any necessary apparel or sea-bedding for the said Apprentice, he and they may deduct any sums properly expended thereon by him or them from the sum so agreed to be paid to the said Apprentice as aforesaid: And the said parties bind and oblige themselves, and their foresaids, to perform the premises to each other under the penalty of £ *10 (ten)* sterling, to be paid by the party failing to the party observing or willing to observe the same over and above performance; providing, that notwithstanding this penal stipulation any Court, Magistrate or Justice of the Peace may exercise such jurisdiction in respect of the said Apprentice as he or they might have exercised if no such stipulation had been herein contained. In witness whereof, *these presents written in so far as not printed by William David Templeton, Clerk, are subscribed by the said parties as follows: viz. by the said H. Hogarth & Sons at Glasgow the sixteenth day of July in the year one thousand nine hundred and forty one before these witnesses: Ian Gillies Donald and William David Templeton Both clerks to H. Hogarth & Sons and by the said George Smith Gunn and Catherine Gunn, at the above address the sixteenth day of July in the year last mentioned before these witnesses: Miss Josie McCulloch (Married Woman) and James McCartney, Joiner.*

Ian G. Donald — Witness

William David Templeton — Witness

Mrs. J. McCulloch (Witness)

J. McCartney. (Witness)

G. S. Gunn.

C. Gunn.

Registered at the Port of

this   day of

Signed

The apprentice's indenture.

During the time in Greenock I learned a lot very quickly. The ship hadn't moved from the berth, but I began to feel and talk like a real sailor.

The cargo was at last discharged, the holds swept and cleaned out, the hatches covered and battened down, and the derricks and running gear stowed. The new crew were signed on to join at one minute past midnight. Leo and I were tired and glad to turn in that night, eagerly looking forward to our first trip to sea

I tossed and turned in the bunk and couldn't get off to sleep as my mind reviewed the past and imagined the future. A loud bang on the cabin door got the three of us up and underway.

The ship left James Watt Dock early in the morning, but not too oearly to prevent the crew of another vessel from leaning out of portholes, rattling plates and spoons to a chorus of 'Roll along you hungry b . . . roll along . . .'. Only one of the deckhands who signed on the previous day reported for duty. He must have been so drunk, he had lost his way. The rest were logged as deserters and shore riggers were employed for the passage to Cardiff via Belfast Lough for convoy down the Irish Sea to the Bristol Channel.

The trip was disappointing. Leo and I had just one visit to the bridge to watch the sobered-up AB steering the ship. Our time was spent cleaning toilets and other compartments which had been used and misused during two weeks in port.

It was becoming quite clear that the navigation and seamanship knowledge absorbed from the pre-sea evening classes and one-year cadet course at the Glasgow Royal Technical College would have to wait to be aired. The affinity between ships' apprentices and toilets washrooms and bilges wasn't well defined in the text book.

The ship arrived at the Queen's Dock Lock in Cardiff at eleven p.m. I was on the fo'csle head with the mate and two riggers. 'I've never been out of Scotland, sir. What's this place Cardiff like?' In the semi-darkness, a wry smile crossed the mate's weatherbeaten face. 'Alright before white man come,' he replied.

As the lock gates were about to open to allow the ship and tugs into the dock, a voice from the bridge shouted. 'Knock off the riggers.' It was just before midnight and they would be due another day's pay after

that. The ship still had to be berthed with just three apprentices, two mates and one AB.

The starboard anchor was let go as the ship surged alarmingly towards the quay wall. An object flew out of the cable locker over the windlass, narrowly missing the mate. It was a chain hook made of two feet of steel bar, used to pull the anchor cable into place as it came down into the locker. I was sent there to help the AB do this when the ship was leaving Belfast Lough, and hadn't disengaged the hook quickly enough to prevent it being trapped by the collapsing links of the huge muddy steel cable. I learned then, anchor cable stowing was to be avoided if possible, to keep well clear of the windlass when the anchor was being dropped, and to report everything.

The mate told us the fourth apprentice would be joining in a couple of days time and the ship would be changing from white to black crew. Bill said it was OK to go from white to black but not the other way round. His reasons would have been unacceptable to the Commission for Racial Equality.

The new captain arrived. He was a senior man in the company and experienced in the operation of Indian-crewed ships. It was immediately apparent he was also experienced in training first trip apprentices.

They started loading cargo on 28 July. There were no deck crew or riggers aboard and we worked all the hours the long summer days and short blackout nights would allow. The cargo was mainly military stores and equipment. Bill reckoned it was for the Middle East, as that was where the war was taking place. It seemed a good guess. We would have to go round the Cape of Good Hope as the Mediterranean was closed to slow convoys. U-boats and surface raiders were wreaking havoc, not only with convoys but with independently-routed ships in the North and South Atlantic and the Indian Ocean. Many were being sunk on the long haul round the Cape and essential supplies for the armies in the Middle East were ending up at the bottom of the sea.

The Indian crew arrived and the look and smell of the *Renfrew* changed. I had never eaten or seen a curry and didn't like the look of it. Bill said, 'You'll soon get used to curry. We have it on white crew ships as well. On them, it's usually lousy but when you are hungry at sea you'll eat anything. There's always curry around on Indian ships and you can go along aft to the crew's galley and have some with a chapatti any time. The officer's cooks here are Goanese. Although they are from India, they have different religious beliefs to the others. Being of Portuguese descent, they can cook and work with beef and pork, which Hindus can't. If you stick the bacon egg and rice cake we get twice a week for breakfast on top of the curry it makes quite a decent plateful. Anyway, it's better than the corned beef you've been used to getting at home on rations. How well we eat on these ships depends on where we are, what it costs, and how much the old man wants to make out of it for himself.'

In all our regular ports they usually have personal financial arrangements with ship chandlers and agents. Those who don't live it up abroad can make enough on a long trip to keep the family without touching their wages. On tramp ships the master is like the owner. There is a story going around that one of them paid the crew off in some remote South American republic, sold the ship, and disappeared. I quite believe it.'

The new Articles of Agreement were opened on 2 August. Bob, the fourth apprentice, and the rest of the officers signed on at Cardiff shipping office. The crew was complete with the exception of the DEMS gunners. They would join at the last minute. The Indians had been transferred from another of the company's ships, then in the UK, and would be repatriated to Calcutta from a convenient port during the voyage. Replacements would be signed on by the agent in Calcutta and conveyed from there to the ship. Tramp steamer changeovers of Indian crews weren't always easy to do in peacetime and during the war it was very difficult indeed. All merchant vessels operated under the Ministry of War Transport and ships'voyages were no longer in the owners' hands.

Bobby's arrival meant an appraisal of our living arrangements. The cabin was about ten feet by eight and used for eating, sleeping, washing and changing. In addition to the three bunks and settee, there was a single wardrobe, four drawers and space for a couple of suitcases under one of the bunks. In the after end of the cabin was the compactum, a very versatile piece of furniture with a mirror, a washbasin with a drop-down lid which served as a table, and space underneath for a galvanised bucket, which directly received the water already used for washing crockery, cutlery or apprentices. There were two portholes. One on the starboard side of the ship opened straight into the top bunk, and the other looked out on to the after deck abreast of number four hatch.

Allocation of individual facilities was easily resolved and a hot-bed policy was agreed.

Bobby was a third-year apprentice, down to earth, easy-going, and only five foot four inches tall. He was prepared to sleep on the settee when necessary.

Bobby was from Ayrshire and went to sea before the war. I asked if he had been torpedoed. 'What's torpedoed? You mean bumped off'. You can always tell a first-tripper when he talks like that. I've been bumped off twice in convoy, first by a U-boat, then bombed off the South of Ireland coming back from Halifax. Luckily, each time we had a grain cargo from Canada. A hit below the waterline on one of these Three Island ships loaded with ore and with the well decks awash, and she's gone in less than a minute. This one's a flush decker and with the cargo we're loading now she won't be down to her marks or anything like it.

'Anyway, Ben, it's not just knowing what to do when you're at sea, it's what to say when you go ashore. You get to learn a lot talking to other seamen. You can soon tell bullshit from the truth. A real sailor always calls the captain the Old Man, but don't let him hear you say it. For us apprentices, there's quite a difference between white and black crew ships. Indians do much of the dirty work we have to do with white crews. The first ship I was bumped off on had a Lascar crew. Talk about panic, it was a miracle we managed to get a lifeboat away. Thank God we were only in it for a couple of days. I still prefer being with Indian crews. They don't go on the booze as soon as the ship gets into port. In fact, they seldom go ashore. What they earn is left at home for the families. I don't think Bill has sailed with them very often. He doesn't seem to know much Hindustani. You can't help but learn it when you are on the ship with them month after month. The one in charge is the Serang. He runs the whole show without doing anything. Next to him is the Tindal, who organises the work. The sailors are called Khalassis. The lamptrimmer is the Kassab and lookoutman the Pouriwallah. Atcha is yes. You've got to learn these names. Just imagine saying 'atcha lookoutman' instead of 'atcha pouriwallah'. It sounds daft. They may call you sahib, but between themselves you're apprentice boy.

My first night ashore in Cardiff was quite memorable. The working arrangements teamed Bobby and me, Bill and Leo. 'You've never been here before, have you?' asked Bobby. I told him this was the first time I had been out of Scotland and according to the mate it was my first foreign port. He said, 'I know it well, we always come here for coal bunkers if possible. Welsh coal is the best in the world. This company's ships are well-known in every port in Wales. The people are nice and friendly, especially the girls if you are in uniform'.

We caught a tram from the Pierhead to town. Bobby suggested going to a dance at the Railwayman's Institute at the far end of Queen Street. First he wanted a beer in the pub opposite. We were admitted into the Institute free, but after a couple of dances Bobby wanted back to the pub. He said the talent in there was better anyway. We landed out in Queen Street in the blackout, in time to catch the last tram down to the docks.

Halfway along Bute Street he wanted another beer. We got off the tram and went into what looked like a fish and chip shop, and were directed through the blackout curtains into a back room with a couple of wooden tables and a few chairs. The curtains parted and another uniformed ship's apprentice came in and sat with us. A large semi-coloured individual put an unlabelled flagon bottle of beer on the table and demanded four shillings. Bob waved him away and said we'd pay when we finished. After he left the room, Bob said, 'We've no money, how about you?' Our new friend produced half a crown. 'Let's finish the beer,' said Bob. 'Just put the money on the table and run when I tell you.' We drank for a while. 'Now,' he said. We tore through the shop into Bute Street, diagonally across to the safer walled side and down towards the Pierhead.

The sound of heavy feet running behind seemed to get closer. We turned the corner and slowed down to a walk to pass the police box at the dock entrance. Safely inside we wished our friend a good trip wherever his ship was bound. On the way to ours Bobby said, 'I'm starving. There's an all-night cafe somewhere here which the dockers use.' I reminded him about the money. He opened his hand and clearly visible in the blackout was a shining half crown piece. 'That fellow has never been at sea for over two years like he said.' 'Why?' I asked. 'He didn't know when to run, and besides a third year apprentice wouldn't have left the money lying on the table.'

Our second and last night ashore together in Cardiff was not uneventful. Bob chose to visit another dodgy establishment in Tiger Bay. He got into conversation with an older man and an attractive young lady who was introduced as his daughter. I left them talking intimately. We had another busy day ahead with a six o'clock start. Leo called me at five forty-five. Bob wasn't on board. He eventually arrived at the ship about nine and told the mate he woke up in a wash-house in a back alley off Bute Street with only his underwear on. He found the rest of his clothes tied in a bundle nearby and couldn't understand what happened but thought he had been drugged.

Even apprentices with three years' seatime behind them didn't always know when to run.

He later said. 'Remember, Ben, in these circumstances always leave your socks on. They won't take them off you, especially if there's holes in them. Because of that I've still got this.' And he took a rolled up ten-shilling note from his pocket.

CHAPTER 2   A Ship at Last: The *Baron Renfrew*

The Renfrew sailed from Cardiff manned and fully loaded on 10 August 1941 to join other ships bound for Freetown. This was my first deep-sea convoy, and being in company with so many other vessels gave me a feeling of security. Deck officers, engineers, radio officers, apprentices and DEMS naval gunners totalled 25 and the balance of a crew of 61 was composed of 35 Indians and one Chinese carpenter.

The convoy system carried over from the First World War had by 1941 generally become the safest way of moving large quantities of supplies and equipment in the North Atlantic. Convoys only operated between the UK, USA and Canada. Many old pre-war ships' masters didn't like them and felt their vessels were safer sailing independently. They hated being told what courses to steer, when to alter, and the minimum speed the ships had to maintain. They felt that trying to keep station in convoy was an unnecessary nuisance, and the commodores in charge of them didn't understand the tramp steamer business as they were either from liner companies or the Royal Navy. Ninety per cent of the ships in most convoys were tramps of one kind or another, which fuelled their argument. However, none of the old masters wanted the jobs themselves.

Atlantic convoys consisted of anything from 40 to 100 vessels. They formed into columns with a minimum of about 600 yards between columns and about 400 yards between ships. Naval escort vessels scurried around like collies coaxing a flock of sheep together, but using loud hailers, Aldis lamps, signalling flags and sometimes even having to resort to semaphore. Small escorts such as corvettes had a dreadful time in Atlantic gales, getting beam on to huge seas as they found themselves continually pitched around during their watching and herding routines. Loaded merchant ships just plodded along at a few knots in much less discomfort.

We arrived at Freetown on 31 August, 17 days after leaving Belfast, the convoy assembly area. During that time Leo and I learned to steer the ship, chip, scrape, wire-brush and red-lead heavily rusted areas of hatch coaming and deck plating. It didn't take long to know how to keep out of the Old Man's line of sight as he regularly perambulated from one side of the lower bridge to the other. Chipping, scraping and all other noisy work was forbidden between one and three in the afternoon. With the exception of the 2nd mate on the Twelve to Four Watch, the other deck officers had a 'lie down'.

Bill and Bob and the two Indian quarter masters worked watch and watch on the bridge until Leo and I were judged suitable to be left at the wheel on our own. This was after the ship left Freetown and was sailing independently. After a masters' convoy debriefing on board Edinburgh Castle permanently anchored there, the ships would sail south unescorted.

Freetown was my first foreign port. There was never any shore leave there for anyone unless they were ill or needed to transfer to another ship. Three days in Freetown was a good induction into tropical climates. With the number of ships arriving and sailing, the bumboats were having a prosperous war. Old clothes, a packet of cigarettes or a plug of tobacco would bring up, on the end of a heaving line, many interesting items from monkeys to mangoes. The warning that mangoes, the most succulent of fruits, were grown in Sierra Leone's mosquito-infested mangrove swamps and carried malaria, didn't deter us from eating as many as we could get. Since leaving home, this was the first fruit we had tasted apart from a shared tin of pineapple chunks. Bill said you couldn't buy mangoes in the UK. They were specially flown out from Africa to some of the top London hotels and cost a bomb. Monkeys were readily available from the bumboats, but like women they were banned on board the ship.

With a mean draft of 22 feet and steaming on Welsh coal, the *Renfrew* averaged her best speed of ten knots for the passage from Freetown down to Cape Town. Any apprehension about being on our own without the company of other vessels was outweighed by the start of regular ship routines. Unfortunately, chipping, scraping and red-leading on deck continued at every possible opportunity. I thought consideration would have been given to U-boat detection systems, but it

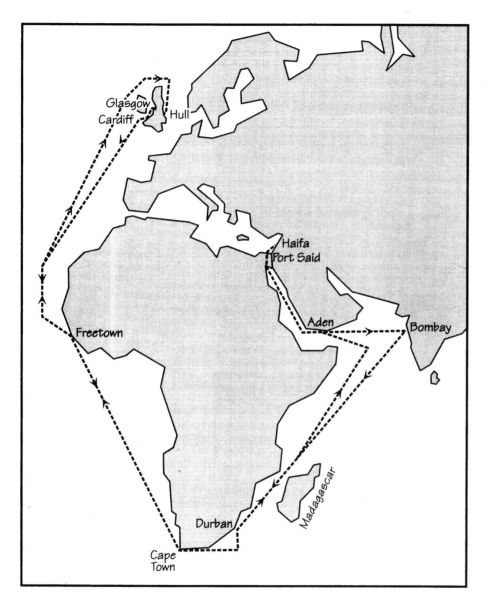

Glasgow
Cardiff
Hull
Haifa
Port Said
Freetown
Aden
Bombay
Madagascar
Durban
Cape
Town

BARON RENFREW

First trip 2 August 1941 to 25 February 1942

Estimated steaming distance 29 400 miles

wasn't, despite the large number of ships lost on this leg of the trip round the Cape to Suez. We were instructed in the use of a flailing electric chipping hammer to give the work more impetus, and this increased the noise level considerably. The defensive armament was an Oerliken anti-aircraft gun on each bridge wing and a four inch on a raised gun platform at the stern of the ship. We had already received instruction in the use of the weapons and the gun's crew was completed with the four apprentices. T. R., who had served in the navy, in the First War said, 'It's no damned good knowing how to do it if you haven't done it.' Paint an empty forty-gallon oil drum the colour of a sub, then chuck it over the side and we'll see what you're like.'

Despite the precise data relayed from the Gunnery Officer (2nd Mate) with his portable range finder on the bridge, it was doubtful whether we could have scored a hit on a battleship, never mind a submarine, and the oil drum disappeared in the distance in a similar condition to when it was 'chucked over the side'. TR wasn't very impressed but charitably told the 2nd Mate that 'they can only get better'. He was right. We did, and scored a direct hit with a four-inch shell twelve months later in the Indian Ocean.

The crew's accommodation underneath the gun platform took the brunt of the firing, while they crouched at the other end of the ship with their fingers in their ears.

The three-watch system four hours on and eight off at sea only applied to bridge duties such as steering and standbys. Field days meant extra work around the decks when required by the Mate. Peggy (chores) for a day included tidying the cabin, queueing for water at the pump, fetching the metal kits of grub from the galley and attending to any confrontation with the cook about their contents. Washing the dishes in a bucket using a minimum of precious fresh water heated up on the galley stove or from the engine room evaporator, with permission from the engineer on watch, was an important part of a peggy. Remembering to fish out the cutlery before throwing the waste water over the side was another. There was no hope of any replacements until the ship arrived at a sympathetic port such as Baltimore or Durban, and one of us could get up the road to the Salvation Army or Missions to Seamen.

Domestic water on tramp ships was strictly rationed and the hand pump in the alleyway was padlocked and opened twice a day by the Chinese carpenter. The weekly ration allowed in the 'Scale of Provisions' was 28 quarts a man per week, except the stokehold hands who were each entitled to an extra quart of water a day when the ship was under steam.

Friction between Chippy and the Indian crew was at its worst when water was being dispensed. They considered he tried to short change them so that his daily tank soundings made good reading for the Mate. Being the keeper of the key Chippy held all the cards and made sure they knew it. As well as drinking cooking and washing, the Indians' meagre ration of water was used for other personal purposes. Class distinction existed between Chippy and the Indians He was considered to be a petty officer and had as little as possible to do with any of them apart from the Serang and Tindal.

The weather was sunny, warm and idyllic through the Doldrums and across the Equator down south to our next port of call. By then we new boys were well drilled in safety procedures at sea in war and peace. The ship was fully blacked out at night. All cabin doors were left open and hooked back into the alleyways and the thick heavily-weighted blackout curtains were kept closed at all times. The only light in a cabin was one red or blue 40 watt bulb covered by an empty can with a hole in the end for the socket. We slept in what was best for getting off the ship in a hurry. Owners of pyjamas only wore them in port. Life jackets were generally recommended as pillows.

The six DEMS gunners were the only enlisted men on board, and apart from naval training this was their first seagoing ship. They weren't professional seamen and all had volunteered for the job. Fred, the gunlayer in charge of the squad, was 22 and came from Battersea in London. He called himself a high-class barrow boy. His local was the Elephant and Castle. Wherever we went ashore in the world, the beer 'was nothing like a pint of the Old Elephant's mild and bitter'. That would be our first stop if the ship ever docked in London. When we eventually got there, the Old Elephant had been bombed. Like the gunners, the radio officers were young and inexperienced. The senior sparks was just 18 years and worked in a distillery in Scotland. Another one drove a bus between Cardiff and Dinas Powis in Wales. We were all in the same boat in more ways than one, which seemed to forge close friendships on board and ashore for many months to come.

The ship was very sparsely stored in Freetown. Well before we reached Cape Town the contents of the icebox smelled every time the second cook removed the padlock and opened it. When there was a following wind, the standby man would have to warn the officer on the bridge before it was opened. The mate would then alter course sufficiently for the foul odours to be blown over the side and away from the captain's cabin. The course would be resumed when all was clear.

Although the weather was fine, it took 17 days to cover the 3,000+ miles to Cape Town. With the known enemy activity in this part of the Atlantic the Old Man had to make many diversionary alterations in accordance with advice received in Freetown and SOS messages from other ships in the area. I didn't know at the time that my best friend Ken, who was mainly responsible for me joining the Merchant Navy, was already missing. His ship, s.s. *Cortona* of Donaldson Line, the owners of *Athenia*, was torpedoed and sunk by a U-boat on his first

Captain T. R. Reid, 'The Old Man', on board the Renfrew, 1941.

trip to sea. This became one of the unexplained mysteries of the war. The two lifeboats were successfully launched. The Captain's boat was eventually picked up with its occupants. The mate's boat which Ken was in disappeared. A long time afterwards a boat similar to it was found washed up somewhere on the West Africa coast, not far from where the *Renfrew* was then. A wristwatch found under one of the thwarts was identified as the mate's. As with all such incidents, many theories evolved, but nothing was ever proved. With the absence of any news from home on long trips, I knew nothing about it until more than a year later.

The statutory 15 days for fresh food to survive in the icebox above the galley was well exceeded by the time we crossed the Equator. A daily ladle of lime juice or lemon juice with sugar was issued by the Steward from a bucket on top of number three hatch. Leo and I were excused the traditional Father Neptune Ceremony when 'crossing the line' for the first time, but were initiated as Limeys. Lime juice was administered to every crew member when the ship was in the Tropics and no fresh food was available. It was defined as an anti-scorbutic. Bill said 'it was hopefully to prevent scurvy'. Bobby added 'and to keep your nature down'.

The ship anchored in Table Bay at 10.30 a.m. on 18 September 1941, just over six weeks after leaving Cardiff. From up on the bridge, Cape Town looked and smelled wonderful. At anchor watch during the night, even better. It was the first time in two years that I had seen a city lit up. I had forgotten what that looked like and realised then how much I had taken it for granted before the war.

Blacking out the ship in port in the UK and all the time at sea was just second nature. Here in Cape Town, everything looked bright and inviting and we couldn't get off the ship quickly enough. It was an exciting thought, made even more so when the Old Man advanced us ten shillings each to go ashore when the ship berthed alongside the quay. Day work and night watch in port limited our shore-going activities to four hours at any one time. We took full advantage of it. Bobby said, 'We're not likely to get into any trouble with only ten bob for three days. He's a bit tight with the money, but I can't ask him for any more or he'll want to know what I am going to do with it, and anyway he'll only say I'm overdrawn and that would be that. It's not worth upsetting him for nothing.'

Leo had a gargantuan appetite and there was no doubt where his ten shillings was going: 'to get something decent to eat and plenty of it'. Dressed in his best go-ashore uniform he found a nice restaurant, told the manager he hadn't had a good meal for two months and what could he have for ten shillings. He was considered to be a deserving case and could have anything on the menu. Leo swore he said everything on the menu and went through the lot. When he started looking at it again the manager thanked him courteously relieved him of the ten shilling note and assured him the offer would never be repeated.

As with Leo, one night in Cape Town saw the end of my ten shillings, but it didn't stop another visit ashore. Luckily, we met two other cadets and were invited on board their ship. This was the first of many visits to other vessels in overseas ports. They usually came about when the subs were spent, a Flying Angel Mission was unavailable and there was nowhere else to go.'

Their vessel was the troopship *Cameronia*, one of Glasgow's transatlantic passenger liners, returning to the UK with German and Italian POWs after landing several thousand British troops at Suez. They had on board a captured U-boat commander. He had sunk his last ship, and was then probably one of the lucky ones who would see the end of the War. Between 1940 and 1945, more than 700 U-boats were lost and few if any of his contemporaries, who had sailed these feared and hated marine assassins from the beginning, survived.

I had fond memories of Cameronia, Transylvania and Athenia. Before the war organised school tours of these ships were made and I had been fortunate to go on board two of them, one being *Cameronia*. They took place the day before sailing for America when the ships were ready for sea. In the galley I remember bakers distributing unlimited quantities of hot rolls to the children.

Our last trip ashore was spent on board an American freighter s.s. *Stella Lykes*. In contrast to the dull grey painted wartime hulls of the ships in British ports and in convoys, *Stella Lykes* was in her peacetime colours with her name in huge white lettering along each side of her shiny black hull. She was discharging general cargo from the States.

Guards patrolled number three hatch. This had a full load of American canned beer. Despite the fact that all US vessels were 'dry', it was a tight squeeze to get into the second engineer's cabin where every compartment including the bunk, wardrobe and wash-basin were packed with beer cans. Leo and I had a great time in Cape Town but had to postpone our sightseeing until 'next trip'.

The weather was good when we left Cape Town on 21 September, but it didn't last long. There was a menacing whisper in the air and the albatrosses seemed to be flying faster than at any time since the ship crossed the line. The 2nd mate said, 'The bottom's fallen out of the glass and we're in for a real blow'. We were, and by the time the Cape of Good Hope was abeam the *Renfrew* was running before, or being blown along by, strong gale force winds and huge confused seas. The short 800-mile passage to Durban began to seem a lot further. The ferocity of the wind seas and swell made it almost impossibe to steer any semblance of a course. I was at the wheel when TR decided to 'bring her round into it and ride it out'. With the wheel hard a-starboard the propeller raced and the whole hull shuddered as the ship was lifted out of the water and dumped back in again. From below there were alarming sounds of crashing and smashing which reached a crescendo when the vessel took it all on the beam and appeared to be going over. The theory that a ship rolling more than of 45 degrees in bad weather would turn over didn't happen on this occasion. Once round and with the engine going ahead sufficiently to stem the force of the wind and seas, the *Renfrew* made it once again.

Damage to the ship was minimal. The lifeboats, although swung out, were still intact, and in Durban when the hatches were opened the cargo was found to be satisfactory. Moveables in cabins, galley, pantry, dining saloon, crew's accommodation and down the engine room and stoke hold took a bit of a beating. One of the seas which struck when the ship was beam-on filled the starboard alleyway and over the storm step into the apprentices' cabin. When I got down from the bridge everything was still floating around. The drawers and the wardrobe had emptied themselves and our gear was being washed for the first time that trip. Leo had more clothes than Bobby and me together and hadn't intended to do any dhobying until it was really necessary. This was an unforeseen set-back to his plans. Bobby reassured us we were safe from U-boats in these conditions and if this ship had been one of those Three Islander he had told us about, we would all be swimming for it now.

With the adverse weather it took six days to get to Durban. The ship needed fresh water, stores and coal. Taking hundreds of tons of bunkers at the Bluff in Durban in sunny hot windy conditions was different to bunkering in Cardiff where the coal was easier to stow and didn't cover the ship from truck to keel. The mate told us Durban was a lovely place, the people were nice and friendly and we were only getting one night ashore each, 'so make the best of it'. We left the ship prepared to do just that. Lots of vessels called at Durban on their way to and from the Middle East and India. The hospitality shown to troops and seamen when they managed to get ashore there could not have been bettered anywhere. During the war it was one of the best places in the world to dock. After a fairly riotous evening, we all looked forward to returning there, but for a longer stay next time.

The following day, the ship's agent told the Old Man that a group of sailors had taken a car and free wheeled down a hill in it the previous night. The mate was suspicious. 'It wouldn't have been you lot, would it?' he asked. I couldn't tell a lie. I told him that I hadn't freewheeled down a hill in a car; I had to stand outside on the running board'. He just laughed. It struck me then that although the war was seldom ever a topic of conversation between us we were all infected with the same live-for-the-day attitude, even the Mate.

The night ashore continued with a rickshaw race through the streets, with three in each one, and the losers to buy the drinks. This was another new experience, clearly not to the rickshaw boys or the onlookers, who sportingly cheered as we passed them. The residents of Durban were not only hospitable, kind and patriotic, but very tolerant as well.

The 3,000 miles from Durban to Aden took 14 days. The ship was still steaming at nine knots. It took about five days to get clear through the Mozambique Channel. The DEMS crew were put on full, continuous gunnery watch. As the narrowest part of the channel is only about 200 miles wide, and all vessels bound for the Middle East had to pass through there, it was an ideal area for enemy activity. On this occasion, there were no distress signals received from other ships and the proposed routeing from there to the Red Sea kept us well out of sight of all land, including the island of Socotra.

We anchored off Aden at 9.00 a.m. on 12 October and left there at noon two days later. One of the gunners was taken ashore by the naval authorities and never rejoined the ship. We were now two short, having put one ashore at Cape Town. There was no possibility of replacements until the ship got back to the UK. The mate asked Fred how four men could manage to keep continuous watches at sea, clean and maintain the guns and equipment and do all the other work for many months ahead. Fred replied, 'We're all in this war together. We'll do longer hours and hope for the best.' DEMS men worked hard, fought hard and played hard, and were respected and admired by seamen throughout the British merchant fleets. In action, the odds were against them: their ships were always the hunted and never the hunter, and they had the unenviable job of trying to protect them. Of the 38,000 DEMS gunners who served on merchant ships during the war 4,000 lost their lives at sea. Our gunlayer's philosophical reply was indicative of the spirit which prevailed all through the service right until the end of hostilities in 1945. They were good shipmates afloat and ashore. I learned a lot about ships' armaments when afloat, and what to avoid when ashore.

The bumboat men in Aden sold Gold Flake and Capstan cigarettes at less than half the duty-free prices on the ship. Bill said they were fakes and Bob reckoned that they were full of saltpetre, but better than the 'C To C' cigarettes sold in South Africa. 'What's "C To C", I asked. 'I think it's Camel To Consumer,' said Bob.

It became continually hotter working on deck and I got burned before I started to tan. Bill told me to go and see the steward and get some camomile lotion, as he looked after the medicine chest and a copy of the *Ship Captain's Medical Guide*. Even if sun-tan and after-sun lotions had been invented by then, they would have been unavailable on tramp ships. He said, 'You go with dirty lady in Durban.' I told him I hadn't gone with any lady there. He showed me the *Guide*, which said: 'Calomel ointment is for some forms of skin disease. In strength of 30 per-cent or over, it kills the germ which causes syphilis. It is therefore a good preventative of syphilis. Used by smearing on the parts.' Only calomel was listed in the steward's *Guide*.

When we arrived in Suez Bay, the first thing we saw was the troopship *Georgic* lying over on her side, having been bombed, set on fire and abandoned. Suez was a convenient point for thousands of troops and military personnel from the UK and from Australia, New Zealand and India to disembark. Unfortunately, it was also a convenient distance from Luftwaffe bases in the Mediterranean. The Georgic was salvaged and towed to India for repair. Many other fine liners weren't so lucky. 557,000 Gross Registered Troopship tons were lost from all causes between 3 September 1939 and the end of June 1943. The number of military personnel and seamen lost was immense. The heaviest was *Lancastria*: only 2,477 rescued from a total of 5310 on board. From a total on board the six worst troop ship sinkings only 5358 were saved.

On most of these vessels troops were jammed down below, often for weeks on end, sailing in dreadful conditions. When the war ended, I did 23 days on a troopship from London to Singapore and had the opportunity to see it first hand. Roughing it on tramships was preferable.

Apprentice George Gunn, 1941.
Christmas Day in the Indian Ocean (in Leo's bridgecoat).

CHAPTER 3 The sinking of HMAS *Sydney*

Everything to do with Port Said was an eye-opener for a first-tripper. The ship was there for five days, discharging and the mate allowed us enough time ashore in the evenings to get to know the place. The vessel lay to both anchors with stern ropes made fast to the quay. Although it was only a short distance ashore, we needed a boat to get on and off. Bumboat men were available at a price. Two of them, Sandy McNab and Jock McKay, were first on board and offered Leo and me a package deal: to be taken in Sandy McNab's boat, then by ghari to the Golden House. He would wait there, take us back to the ship, and next day bring us each a fez and a box of turkish delight. Anything spent in the Golden House was an optional extra. Strangely, the price was ten shillings – exactly what we were to get for the stay in port. I didn't take him up on it, but helped Leo dispose of his turkish delight the following day.

Despite his name and self-proclaimed honesty, Sandy McNab was in every other way a Gyppo. He was well known to all British ships calling at Port Said and had made periodic trips to the UK before the war, visiting the offices of some of the regulars. All hands seemed to feel he was as trustworthy as any other citizen of that part of the world.

My ten shillings still intact, I got a free lift ashore with the ship chandler who put me in a ghari for the Golden House. I had arranged to meet three of the DEMS gunners, Fred Gordon and Lofty at this 'palace of arts'. Previously I had asked Bobby about our Company Indentures, which said, 'the Apprentice shall not frequent Taverns or Alehouses or Houses of Ill-Repute, unless on their business.' 'That doesn't matter,' he replied, 'it says frequent, we never get ashore often enough to frequent anywhere.'

I thought the ship chandler's rapid-fire instructions to the ghariwallah must have been mistaken because I was first taken to a place called the French House. It was evident that houses in Port Said were different to those in Glasgow. It was a sleazy-looking joint, but probably paying more commission. I hadn't been at sea long enough to know about these things, but I was learning fast. My three shipmates, among dozens of soldiers sailors and airmen waiting to go to war, were in an advanced state of enjoyment when I eventually arrived at the Golden House. Port Said *** and **** brandies were taking their toll. All I had read about San Francisco and the Barbary Coast in sailing ship days seemed to be happening in the Golden House in Port Said in 1941. I was late getting there, most of the action had already happened and my shipmates were running out of cash. The place was teeming with girls of every colour and nationality. 'You missed the exhibition, Ben, and I'm ruddy annoyed about it,' said Lofty. The only exhibitions I had ever been to were held in the Kelvin Hall and the art galleries in Glasgow, but this was obviously different. I asked him why he was annoyed and he said, 'The girl I had before it started turned out to be one of the two performers and I now feel kind of inadequate.'

'Never mind,' said Fred 'you'll get over it. She's probably forgotten by now who you were anyway.'

The second night in Port Said was somewhat different. As soon as I stepped ashore, an Arab urchin shouted, 'Mister you want girls, drinky-dancy or picture house, me take you.' I opted for the picture house. After jogging behind him through a maze of ill-lit streets and alleyways, he found it. I had a feeling that we went through some of them more than once, but was relieved when I entered and found it really was a cinema. The long wooden backless forms, similar to the front seats in the Standard in Partick, were crammed. I squeezed in between two of the Arab audience and waited for the picture to start.

In view of what I already knew about Port Said, I wondered what kind of pictures would be shown. The lights went out and to wild applause from the audience the *Great Dictator*, with Charlie Chaplin as Adolph and Jack Oakie as Il Duce, started. It was surprising that the film made it to Egypt. It was a fairly recent production and I was amazed to see it for the first time in Port Said in the middle of a war. The language was English, with French subtitles, and down one side of the screen Arabic, and down the other, Greek. The various interpretations weren't quite synchronised and Arab-, Greek-, French- and English-speakers saw the jokes or shouted at Hitler or Mussolini at

Port Said Catholic Church.

Port Said Post Office.

Port Said, general view.

different times. It seemed a good film, and I resolved to see it again where audience participation wouldn't be paramount, and quite so vocal. Going to the pictures in Port Said was another unique experience. My guide was waiting outside, but his further offer of girls or drinky-dancy was again refused.

The return trip was quicker than the outward one. That was the last time I went ashore at night on my own in Port Said. It was interesting, but not worth the risks.

The Golden House prospered for about another year before British and Aussie troops on their way to Alamein and the Western Desert said farewell, then burned it down.

Our work on board during the stay in Port Said was divided between oiling winches, going up and down the holds protecting the cargo from over-attention by the Egyptian dockers and cleaning and cement-washing the insides of the domestic fresh water tanks in number four 'tweendeck. Each tank held eleven tons of water and was built into one of the hottest parts of the ship. With no refrigerator of any kind, there was no hope of a cold drink on board at sea or in port. After cleaning, flushing out and refilling the tanks, we were told by the mate that the cementy taste of the water would go, and that anyway, it was good for our systems.

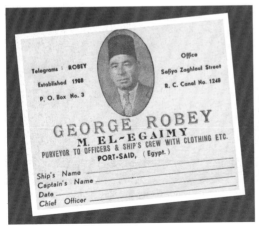

Calling card from local trader or 'bumboat man'. The name has been taken from a famous music hall comedian of the time. Other Egyptian traders, with an eye for Scottish customers, called themselves Sandy McNab and Jock Mackay.

The ship left Port Said for Haifa at 5.00 p.m. on 26 October and arrived there two days later, a couple of feet lighter due to the cargo discharged in the Egyptian port. The weather was good and sunny. At that time, many British cargo vessels carrying military stores and equipment plied up and down the 174 miles between Port Said and Haifa in comparative safety. German forces and resources were fully employed defending their gains along the coast in North Africa and attacking Malta.

The difference between Port Said and Haifa, Egypt and Palestine, was apparent as soon as the ship berthed. There was no dockside hassle, no bumboat men selling their wares, and everything looked clean and tidy. I was anxious to get ashore in the Holy Land to see if the Bible was correct. Although they lived in the same city, the division between Jews and Arabs was clear. The Jews weren't inclined to be friendly to visitors, but their side of the street was the better of the two. Nevertheless, we had an enjoyable two weeks there. The cinemas were good, and during the intervals we ate lots of corn on the cob and ice-cream. This was a real treat, as was the cold jaffa juice from freshly-pressed oranges, sold in shops and cafes. To hard-up ships' apprentices, good nights ashore in Haifa were pleasant and very cheap.

Troops waiting to be drafted to Egypt seemed to find Haifa rather quiet and sober, particularly Anzacs who had previously sampled the delights of Port Said. They were great fighters and popular when they got to the Western Desert. The local Jews didn't entirely regret their departure. On our way back aboard one evening, we stopped at a cafe outside the dock gates. The place was empty until some Aussies entered. They took exception to something the owner said, picked up a large water-boiler off the counter and threw it across the room. When they started to wreck the rest of the cafe, we left. Even Bobby's usual fighting spirit was suppressed. He just said, 'Wasn't that bloody awful, Ben.'

Our cargo was urgently required. British and Allied forces were fighting rearguard battles just along the coast in Egypt and Libya, victory was in the balance and the troops needed all the equipment, supplies and reinforcements they could get. Every available British cargo vessel and troopship was deployed to that end. Cargo was worked

HMAS *Sydney* sinking the Italian cruiser *Bartolomeo Calleoni* northwest of Crete, 19th July 1940. Shells throw up a line of water along the ship's side. Photo taken from *Sydney*.

(*Imperial War Museum*)

Bartolomeo Calleoni (reputed to have been the fastest cruiser in the world with a speed of 41 knots) – ablaze with her bow blown off. Photo taken from *Sydney*.

around the clock, but it still took two weeks to discharge. One apprentice was on night-watch and the others helped the mates look after the holds, the winches and deck work. We were each given one full day ashore, so Leo and I used ours for a trip to Nazareth.

Dressed in whites and sporting epaulettes, we went by local bus. A single decker with solid tyres and dirt track roads made the short journey seem quite long. All the other passengers were Arabs. It was jam packed, the weather was hot and we stood and sweated all the way. It must have been market day in Haifa as most of them had stores, live chickens and all sorts of other baggage never seen on Glasgow Corporation Transport. They all took turns to shout at the driver but he didn't seem to mind and just shouted back. The bus stopped frequently to drop off and pick up passengers, birds and animals, and for roadside toilet purposes. Intending passengers who couldn't get on board because the bus was full, screamed abuse at the driver. He just smiled, closed the door and drove on to the next enforced stop. It must also have been market day in Nazareth, as the contents of the bus on return were similar. Getting on board was every man for himself, and Leo's size weight and rugby experience were used to our advantage.

Camels, souvenir-sellers and guides who were well-versed in the Holy Bible made an interesting day away from the ship. I was assured by our little Arab guide that the leaf he gave me was from the same tree as the Crown of Thorns for Jesus. I couldn't really doubt him. It has survived another 58 years pressed between the pages of my Boys' Brigade Bible.

When we went back aboard that evening, a warship had berthed on the opposite side of the quay. By the time we turned to in the morning, it had sailed. Bill had been on night-watch and said it had only come in for bunkers stores and water, and one of the crew told him the name of the ship was *Sydney*, an Australian light cruiser. The seaman also said they had previously sunk an Italian ship, supposed to have been the fastest cruiser in the world. Because so many major British Naval disasters followed within weeks, the sinking of battleships *Queen Elizabeth* and *Valiant* by the Italians in Alexandria Harbour, and *Prince of Wales* and *Repulse* by the Japanese in the Pacific, HMAS *Sydney* sailing from Haifa on 7 November was easily forgotten. That is, until I

read Michael Montgomery's 1981 book, *Who Sank The Sydney?*. Montgomery's father was one of the deck officers on the ship when she was reputedly sunk by *Kormoran*, a German armed raider, on 19 November 1941. According to the book, there were several unexplained events concerning the loss of the ship with its entire crew of 645 men. It would considerably add to them if the ship we saw in Haifa on 6-7 November was the *Sydney*. If not, what similar vessel could have been there at that time, and why should the seaman tell Bill it was *Sydney*?

Neither Mr. Montgomery nor Ludovic Kennedy, who wrote the preface to the book, are satisfied that all questions about the loss of the ship have been answered. Ludovic Kennedy writes 'The book is a fascinating and unusual piece of naval detection, and one can only deplore the attitude of the Australian naval authorities over the years in being so unnecessarily secretive. Have they also somethingto hide?'

Of the 32 dates in the book showing *Sydney*'s movements in the Indian and Pacific Oceans in 1941, only one of them would preclude the ship being at Haifa on 7 November, namely a reference to Fremantle on the eleventh. It is assumed that the dates came from the Australian naval authorities mentioned in the book and were related in some way to the vessel's log book entries. Men who sailed on, and were in charge of, ships during the war know that log books did not always record exactly what happened. This was often for security reasons, and also when books were to be examined by a party not directly involved with the operation of a vessel. Log books have also been used to lay false trails.

Should *Sydney* have made another trip to the Middle East for undisclosed reasons and sailed from Haifa on return 6-7 November, she could easily have made the passage from there to a position 300 miles north of Geraldton, in Australia, for an encounter with *Kormoran* and/or another vessel on 19 November.

The passage from Haifa through the Canal and past Aden would take about four days. Full-away after Suez at an economical speed of about 25 knots would put the ship to a position off the western entrance to Sunda Straight on 17 November, as shown in the book; then heading for Fremantle on a directly opposite course to *Kormoran*, where the two ships supposedly met on the nineteenth.

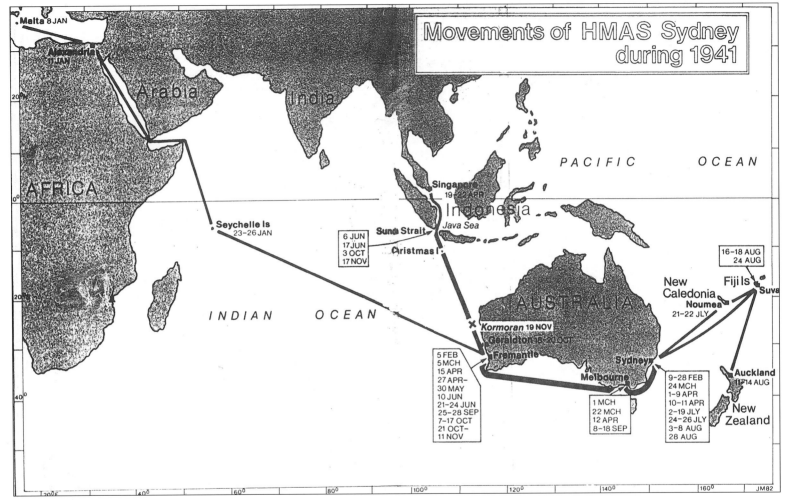

Movements of HMAS *Sydney* during 1941.

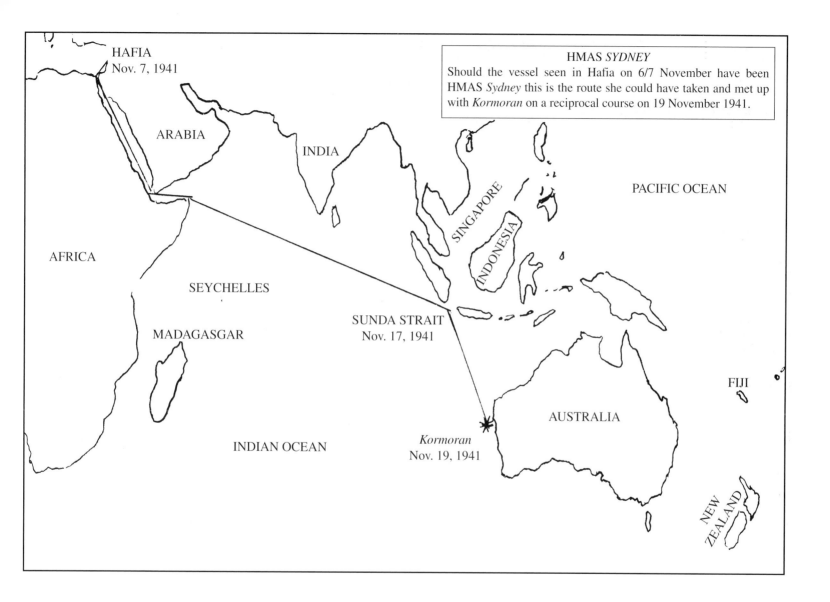

HAFIA
Nov. 7, 1941

ARABIA

INDIA

AFRICA

SEYCHELLES

MADAGASGAR

SINGAPORE

INDONESIA

PACIFIC OCEAN

SUNDA STRAIT
Nov. 17, 1941

INDIAN OCEAN

Kormoran
Nov. 19, 1941

AUSTRALIA

FIJI

NEW ZEALAND

HMAS *SYDNEY*
Should the vessel seen in Hafia on 6/7 November have been
HMAS *Sydney* this is the route she could have taken and met up
with *Kormoran* on a reciprocal course on 19 November 1941.

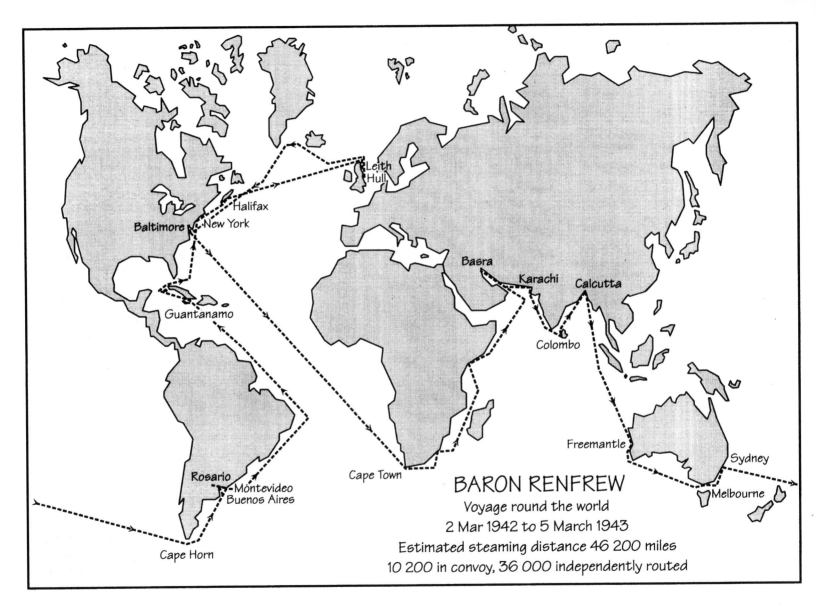

Leith
Hull
Halifax
Baltimore
New York
Guantanamo
Basra
Karachi
Calcutta
Colombo
Freemantle
Sydney
Cape Town
Rosario
Montevideo
Buenos Aires
Melbourne
Cape Horn

BARON RENFREW
Voyage round the world
2 Mar 1942 to 5 March 1943
Estimated steaming distance 46 200 miles
10 200 in convoy, 36 000 independently routed

Even if this were ever proved, the mystery will remain as to why *Sydney* returned to the Mediterranean, what secret mission she was assigned to and by whom, and what ship eventually disposed of her if it wasn't *Kormoran*. Or will the disappearance of *Sydney* without trace remain just another unsolved tragedy of the war at sea?

With the remainder of her cargo discharged, the *Renfrew* left Haifa on 12 November for Port Said, Suez and Bombay, a distance of about 4,000 miles, and arrived there on the 28th, with a light 12-foot draft. Getting to India had always been a career ambition. Even after such a short time, it was clear the only real way to see the world was from the deck of a tramp steamer. Long turn-around periods in port, with general cargo as was landed in Port Said and Haifa, presented the right opportunities. Cargo loading and discharging equipment and facilities both ashore and aboard vessels had changed little since before the First World War. Manhandling derricks winches old wooden hatch boards tarpaulin covers and wedges throughout the working day, added a great deal to the loading and unloading times in ports. It was real sailoring: what we signed on to do. We enjoyed the work on board and the time ashore. It was clear by then why the company indentures didn't contract to make officers of us, although they certainly made us seamen.

At the wheel early one morning on the 4-8 a.m. watch, I reported to the mate that I could see a ship's masthead light dead ahead. He ordered me to alter course ten degrees to starboard. We were then off Perim Island, at the entrance to the Red Sea, and day was breaking. The lights were coming up fast and he shouted from the wing of the bridge for me to alter ten degrees more. It was *Queen Mary* and *Queen Elizabeth* in line ahead, sailing full speed for Suez with thousands of Australian troops on board. Their bow waves and wash struck the *Renfrew* on the port side, and because of her light trim caused the biggest roll since the Cape of Good Hope. The Old Man bounded up on the bridge shouting, 'What the hell's that?' Mr Gibson, in his usual imperturbable way, said 'Just the two Queens in a hurry' 'I hope they don't get the same kind of reception as the poor old *Georgic*' said TR.

The opening of the Suez Canal in 1870 established Bombay as the gateway to India. Trade with Europe flourished and Bombay boomed. When we stepped ashore there in 1941, opulence and poverty still co-existed, with one dependent on the other. Much of what we had seen in the cinemas at home and what we were encouraged to read about in school books was right there. Looking at Bombay for the first time from the deck of a cargo ship I could well understand why so many films had been made about India. The mystique generated by pictures like *Lives of a Bengal Lancer* and *Clive of India* was readily apparent. Ghandi's struggle to get rid of the British didn't make much sense to me at the time. Many Indians prospered from our influence; many more didn't. That remained unchanged for another 50 years, and as with other former British overseas possessions, the future is still uncertain.

We stayed in Bombay for seven days, loading part cargo for the UK and sailed on 5 December. During that time, each apprentice was allowed two afternoons ashore. Bobby knew the place quite well and offered to take me sightseeing. He wasn't sure of the names of any temples, mosques or other beautiful buildings we passed in the ghari. After a quick trip around the city he said that he wanted a chokli, and told the ghariwallah to take us to Grant Road. I hadn't heard the word chokli before, but I knew that it had nothing to do with eating or drinking. I remained in the ghari at Grant Road and Bob returned in less than half an hour, one rupee lighter and with a satisfied look. He never mentioned it again and I didn't need to ask.

The ghariwallah wanted an extra rupee for waiting, but Bob would only pay for the ride so we had to walk back. He knew a shortcut into the docks, but unfortunately it was through a prohibited area and one of the armed guards arrested us, then locked us up. It was a couple of hours before the 3rd Mate arrived with some ship's papers to prove who we were.

One day out from Bombay, heading for Durban, Sparks received a radio message saying the Japanese had bombed Pearl Harbour. When I asked where that was, I was told that it was somewhere in the Pacific and that all British ships had to put into the nearest port. We arrived back in Bombay and were told the message had been sent in error, so we set out once more for Durban. TR was really annoyed at the loss of time and gave the Sea Transport Officer (STO) a few tips on how to run a war.

The delay had quite an effect on his plans for this long, rather dangerous 4,000 mile passage. In Bombay, we took on the bare amount of stores and bunkers to get to Durban. For religious, and no doubt economic reasons, there was no fresh meat or vegetables, and Indian coal was guaranteed to reduce the ship's speed by up to two knots. This made it harder for the engineers, firemen and trimmers to maintain a decent head of steam. The day's run each noon looked progressively worse so the ship would still be somewhere in the Indian Ocean on Christmas Day.

The day before that, I had gone into the galley and found the second cook washing down a hairy object in a basin of Condy's Fluid. To me, it looked like a half-drowned Persian cat. When I was told, however, that it was the meat for Christmas Eve dinner, I decided that I would give it a miss. The icebox was emptied, cleaned out,and left open until the ship arrived in Durban. For the first time in the Tropics, with a following wind, it wasn't necessary for the officer of the watch to alter course for the opening of the icebox to avoid the smells getting up to the bridge and into the Captain's cabin.

A barrel of salt beef was opened on Christmas Day and that, with a portion of haricot beans and a potato, provided the main course. We lined up outside the cabin to be wished the compliments of the season by TR, immaculately turned out in whites and war ribbons. We had clean shirts and clean hands. The chief steward, carrying a bottle of sherry and a glass, accompanied him and the mate. Greetings were exchanged and our glass of sherry was downed. 'Just like giving strawberries to donkeys. You'll enjoy your dinner; it's salt beef fresh out of the barrel and tastes like chicken.' They left to continue their rounds and the steward followed with the sherry and the glass.

Although the loaded draft and trim of the ship were better than any time so far during the trip, she rolled and pitched heavily all Christmas Day in monsoon-like weather. Everything was against her, but the Mate said we would definitely be in Durban by New Year's Day, and have a real good dinner on board. We looked forward to that and made the best of the barrel beef. Before it was cooked, no two pieces looked like they came from the same animal. Bill said it wasn't beef; it was salt horsemeat, not the horse itself but what it ate.

Having made a good friend of the bhandari (crew's cook) by regularly eating his curry rice and chapattis, Leo had no problem filling up after, with the salt horse and a whole enamel cooking dish of pudding made with sago or rice and watered-down Nestlé's Condensed Milk. He always asked before starting, 'Does anyone else want some of this? If not I'll have it. 'Until then, home-style milk puddings were too fresh in my memory to touch it. Leo's periodic flatulance didn't bother him like it did the rest of us in the close confines of our ten by eight foot cabin. Essential air changes were often provided by two fully-open portholes and the cabin door hooked right back into the alleyway.

TR waylaid me on the way up to the wheel and asked when I'd last had a haircut. He took a six-inch rule from his pocket, pulled my hair up and measured it, then asked who cut it. I told him we cut each other's. 'Get Chippy to do it, he's good with the tools, and tell him to do the rest of you lot as well while he's at it. I'll inform the mate and he will put it on Chippy's maintenance list with the windlass hatch covers and the fresh water pump. We're docking in Durban soon and I don't want you and your pals going ashore from here looking like a bunch of Fuzzy-Wuzzies. This company's ships are regular traders to Durban and so am I, and we're all welcome visitors, so remember it. That order includes using other people's motor cars without permission. When you go to the wheel now, steer a good straight course I'll be watching your wake from here.'

A full Lascar crew change took place in Bombay. The new crowd joined from Calcutta and an entry was made in the official log book dated 30 November 1941: 'This is to certify that Shipping Master boarded today to check Lascar crew advances given abroad. Also balance of wages due them before crew were sent back to Calcutta for final discharge and payment of wages. Their wages were made up to 3.12.41 being the date of their arrival in Calcutta.'

Chippy, the Chinese carpenter, signed on again and stayed with the ship. This was welcome news. He was a good worker and Indian handler and also cut up my Scotch Cake, Cornucopia or Fair Maid plugs of pipe tobacco. At four shillings for one pound out of bond they were an affordable smoke. Chippy saw me paring them down with a knife and said, 'This no good. Me do it better.' He sat on his trestle with the plug of tobacco under his foot, steadied it with his hand and sliced it down to half an inch using a two-foot long narrow wooden plane.

The piece he couldn't cut was his. 'Velly dangelous when ship rolls, Ben,' so we agreed on one inch.

We arrived Durban on the afternoon of 30 December and were all glad to get there after a long slow passage of 23 days. The average speed of the ship was seldom more than 7½ knots. Just before Christmas Bobby had complained of head pains. TR examined him and the entry in the official log book reads: 'Apprentice Robert B. Scott reports a shooting pain behind the left ear. No swelling is visible but on pressure being applied a minute growth is felt. Hot formentations applied and patient off duty'.

The day after we docked, the following log book entry was made: 'Apprentice Robert B. Scott was taken ashore to ear specialist who then examined him thoroughly. He stated that said apprentice was suffering of after effects of Mastoid trouble. Medical forms issued and apprentice Robert B. Scott was admitted to hospital'.

On 3 January the last log book entry on Bob reads, 'This is to certify that Apprentice Robert B. Scott was paid off, his personal effects being left at Custom House. The balance of wages deposited at shipping office which amounted to £18.0.5. His Unemployment Card stamped to date which equalled 22 weeks and was handed over to Shipping Master. N. H. to be paid on arrival at UK.'

Bobby's last night ashore was on the day we arrived in Durban. Although he didn't feel well and had been 'climbing the cabin bulkhead' that didn't stop him from having a final fling. On the way back aboard, for no apparent reason he put his fist through a large shop front window which fell to bits at our feet. Before the ship sailed on 7 January, we were each given an afternoon off to visit him in hospital. He was to undergo further operations. The doctor told him the mastoids were the result of blows to the head and his amateur boxing days were over.

Being master of a tramp steamer in 1941 didn't just involve navigation ship handling and seamanship. He was lawyer, doctor, nurse and sometimes surgeon. His authority was absolute and unquestioned and the responsibilities immense, particularly in wartime. TR had every quality to run a happy and efficient ship, but never to the detriment of rigid discipline.

The ship stayed in Durban for eight days, working cargo, bunkering and taking on board much-needed stores and real fresh water. The return trip independently to Freetown and from there convoy back to the UK would take about six weeks. Apart from topping up the domestic water tanks, it was in the interests of the ship, the captain's resources and the crew's health that only absolute necessities were taken on board at Freetown. We would, of course, take another chance on the mangoes.

New Year's Eve in Durban wasn't unlike Hogmanay in Glasgow, and you didn't need to be Scottish to celebrate. Never having been out of Scotland I was surprised by that, although everyone we met during the evening and throughout the night apparently had some family or ancestral connections there.

Our arrival coincided with news that the battleships *Prince of Wales* and *Repulse* had been lost. This caused a great deal of shock to the residents of Durban. They knew the ships well. The first we heard of the tragedy was on arrival there three weeks after it happened.

There was no work on New Year's Day. I went ashore on my own in the morning and finally succumbed to Durban hospitality in the Marine Club. After a sumptuous South African buffet and a convivial dose of John Barleycorn, I fell asleep in one of the armchairs. The Club was hosted by the ladies of Durban and run on a voluntary basis for lonely seamen ashore in the Port. Instead of someone banging on my bunkboard on board the ship and telling me I'd got ten minutes to get up on the bridge, I was gently encouraged to come to, as the floor was required for a New Year's dance. That's when I met Dorothy, who had tried unsuccessfully to push the chair clear. After dancing with her all evening, then a lift back to the ship in her father's car, I had no regrets at missing 'the best New Year dinner ever on the *Renfrew*'. The kind offer for father to pick me up in the car and take us both to the cinema the following evening was readily accepted.

An apprentice in uniform going to the pictures in a chauffeur-driven car with a beautiful girl in the back seat couldn't go unnoticed by my shipmates. They arranged themselves along the rail at the top of the gangway and did their best to simulate a wedding send-off. I was embarrassed, but Dorothy and her father seemed to enjoy it.

Dinner at Umgeni, in the opulence of a beautiful villa and served by a large Zulu dressed in a leopard skin, was a Sunday treat for Leo and me. Dorothy had asked if another apprentice would like to come along for a meal. Leo was the best bet for serious eating and didn't need coaxing. I still hadn't come to terms with shipboard curry, but what they served there was different. Two chickens were segmented, cooked and reassembled in the skins and Leo was hungry enough to ensure there was nothing left over.

We sailed from Durban on 7 January and arrived Freetown 16 days afterwards. The ship stayed there for four further days waiting for a slow enough convoy before sailing homeward bound for the UK. The passage was uneventful and the deep sea convoy dispersed at Oban on 17 February. The discharge port was to be Hull via Methil, and this meant two coastal convoys to get there. Extra gunners were taken on board for these convoys. They were mainly army men and signed on the articles as deckhands, like the vessel's regular naval seamen. Their services weren't used on this occasion, and the ship arrived at Hull in good condition on 24 February 1942.

Selfishly, I had forgotten the severe wartime conditions which existed in Britain when we left seven months previously. Going ashore in Hull that winter was a vivid reminder. Shortages, rationing, bombing and other personal sacrifices had intensified considerably. I was struck by the stoic resistance and fighting spirit which prevailed everywhere and I was sorry for those who had to stay there and take it. They, in turn, were sorry for us going to sea. All being well we would get home for a few days leave before sailing again. Before we could, however, some dhobying was required and at least one shirt needed to be ironed. The trouble was that we didn't own an iron. In the event, a lemonade bottle filled with boiling water served to press the creases out of the collar and cuffs and make us look presentable.

CHAPTER 4   Voyage around the World 1942-3

The crew signed off and new articles were opened on the 26 February. The ship was required to put to sea again as soon as possible and home leave was restricted to a couple of days. Bill was transferred to another vessel and the apprentice vacancies were filled by two Johns, Ellerby and Hunter, both first trippers. Seniority entitled Leo and me to the best bunks, and the new boys were left to argue over the settee. Only the captain, the chief and 2nd. engineer and two gunners, Bill the Newfoundlander and Fred from Battersea, signed on for the next trip. We heard on the 'galley wireless' that it would be a short one across to the States and back to the UK in less than three months, with the possibility of longer leave at the end.

In addition to discharging the cargo, a number of repairs and improvements were made to the ship. Both lifeboats were 'pully-haully', needing to be manhandled and steered with oars, so one of them was fitted with an engine. Unfortunately, they forgot to allow for the extra weight and when the boat was winched up to boat deck level, the after manilla ropefall parted and the two shipyard men delivering the boat plunged 40 feet down into the cold muddy water of Alexandra Dock.

They were pulled out, brought back on board, wrapped up in ship's blankets and sat in front of the galley fire with a bottle of the Old Man's favourite scotch. He was ashore at the time.

With their clothes dry and a couple of cups of coffee to wash down the whisky, they made for the gangway. 'You chaps will be going home now,' said the 2nd. Engineer. 'Home?' said one of them. 'We're going back to the Yard. Don't you know there's a war on?'

Merchant ships were continually being upgraded to improve defence and for the protection of survivors in lifeboats and rafts against extreme cold and heat. A long stay in port would give rise to all sorts of (usually anonymous) ideas for improvements. In Hull, it was large machines for making fresh water from salt water. Each one came with two crates of patent fuel, with one set for each boat. Before the ship sailed, an unwritten standing order from the mate was 'the first man in the boat will throw the lot over the side to make room for the crew'. A sinking ship would periodically have to get two lots of survivors into one boat and there was no room for orange boxes and a water distillery, especially in the North Atlantic, summer or winter.

Standing at George Square in the blackout waiting for a tram which never came was another vivid reminder of bleak wartime conditions I had forgotten about for many months. It was only ten o'clock and the streets of Glasgow were deserted. Walking home, carrying a kitbag of dirty washing and a few pounds of precious sugar, I passed the Anchor Line offices and remembered, what seemed a long time ago, standing reading a notice on a board outside giving details of the sinking of the *Athenia* on 3 September 1939, the day war was declared.

I spent two days at home visiting friends and relatives, and then it was back down to Hull on the return half of my travel warrant. Ashore, newspaper and radio reports of the carnage being suffered by the Merchant Navy seemed exaggerated. At any rate, that's what I wanted to believe and couldn't get back to the ship quickly enough. Half of the cargo had been discharged and pre-First World War ack-ack guns were being replaced with pre-Second World War ones. I was selected to go for a two day course on the use of Marlin machine guns.

We were picked up by truck and delivered with crew members of other ships to a Nissen hut in a field somewhere outside Hull. The mate said he expected us to return as qualified gunners. We would be given something to eat and five shillings for the two days. We could keep the money. Then he added, 'The way you lot get treated ashore in uniform, that should be enough for two good nights' drift'.

The bits on theory and stripping down, cleaning and oiling were passable. Hitting a long sleeve towed by a hedge-hopping bi-plane, flown by an intrepid RAF pilot, wasn't. Sailors and firemen, cooks and stewards, galley boys and apprentices, all firing at the same moving target at the same time prompted remarks about winning the DFC and being posted to a Spitfire Squadron as light relief. We all got the gunnery certificate and, as you might expect, we spent the money in the traditional way.

MERCHANT NAVY A/A GUNNERY COURSE.

CERTIFICATE OF PROFICIENCY.

H/584

Date stamp of Training Centre.

(2 DAY'S COURSE)

Name...... *Gunn G.*

Rank or Rating...... *Cadet.*

B. of T. or D.B. No......

has completed the Merchant Navy A/A Gunnery Course and is qualified in the firing and ~~Knowledge of a~~ Cleaning & Oiling of :- *Marlin*

machine gun.

W.E. Griffiths

Rank...... *Leutenant RN*

D.E.M.S. Training Centre......

George Gunn's gunnery proficiency certificate.

42

Air raids in Hull had the same effect as air raids in Glasgow: everything stopped, including public transport. I started walking the long road back to the ship but, like others that night, ended up a guest of the Salvation Army. The people staying there came from all walks of life and the place was full to capacity. We each had a hot drink and the use of a camp bed and a blanket for the night. Some seemed regular visitors and readily offered advice. I took notice of it, kept my clothes and shoes on, and left nothing lying about as I was told it would be gone in the morning. When everyone had settled down and all the bunks were full, the lights were put out and a large galvanized bucket placed inside the door. It was well used during the night, until someone tripped over it and flooded a large area of the floor. Colourful comments from around the room ensured there was no more sleep. I learned then of the good work of the 'Sally Ann' and what they had to put up with.

After 15 days in Hull, we weren't sorry to sail. The ship left on 12 March in a coastal convoy, bound for Loch Ewe via Methil. A light ship in the North Atlantic in winter wasn't the best guarantee of a comfortable passage across to the States. The trim of the ship was improved with quantities of shale ballast loaded in a couple of the holds The latest idea for vessels in coastal convoys was to fly personal barrage balloons. These were to be flown from ships at specified heights to deter Nazi divebombers. The large balloons, sprouting up around towns and cities, were launched and controlled under different conditions to those on ships yawing all over the place in bad weather. Our efforts to launch it from the top of number 2 hatch resulted in wrapping it round the wheelhouse window, preventing those on the bridge from following the ship ahead. TR's orders to stow it away so he never saw it again were happily carried out. We anchored in Loch Ewe on 17 March without seeing any Nazi dive bombers, and awaited convoy instructions.

I was on standby in the gunners' quarters playing pontoon when word came from the bridge that, due to increased enemy action in the Atlantic, two extra gunners, put on board for the coastal passage, were to sail with the ship. One of them starting sobbing about his wife and children waiting at home and claimed that he had to get off. Fred looked up from his cards and said, 'That's easy. Just go up on the bridge and tell the Old Man to go and F . . . himself and you'll be off before you know it.'

Two coastal convoys (some with barrage balloons) passing port-to-port, 1944-5. Photograph taken from the Escort vessel HMS *Viceroy*.

An outward bound North Atlantic convoy – under protection of Coastal Command aircraft which played a major part in winning 'The War At Sea'. They escorted 4,947 merchant ship convoys; attacked 587 U-boats and flew more than 55 million miles between 3rd September and 30th September 1942.

(*Imperial War Museum*)

Shortly after, there were loud blasts on a pea whistle. I ran up on the bridge. A voice called out 'Boy, hoist a signal on that halyard and tell the MPs to get on board here urgently.' Two MPs arrived, saw TR then frog-marched the Army gunner to the rope ladder. When he was about ten feet from the bottom one of them 'accidentally' stepped on his hands. He fell on his back into the boat, and as it left looked up with a large smile on his face.

Most of the vessels in the large convoy were in ballast, and columns of ships stretched right out to the horizon. It was the third winter of the war and, after two weeks in the UK, it was clear food rationing could hardly get worse. By March 1942, Doenitz and his U-boat packs were decimating Allied shipping in the Atlantic. Most of the 80 or 90 vessels in that convoy would sail for home ports, heavily loaded with food and other essentials. But how many would get there? It was seldom a topic of conversation on board, and seamen had no idea then of the number of ships being lost. Between the beginning of February 1941 and the end of 1942 more than 350 ships were sunk in the Atlantic between Greenland and New York. Much of this could have been prevented if Admiral Ernest J. King, the Chief of US Naval Operations, had agreed earlier to coastal convoys up and down the eastern seaboard.

One morning, at daybreak, we were surprised to find the convoy steaming through ice. The ships were like large dark stains on a white tablecloth, and we seemed to be somewhere inside the Arctic Circle between Iceland and Greenland. For days before that, vessels rolled and pitched in typical winter north Atlantic weather. None of these conditions was suitable for U-boat operations. It was an ill wind etc., and much appreciated.

The first trippers were introduced to their new careers in the best possible manner. By the time we got to Baltimore, they would know whether or not they had chosen the right job. They were learning fast, although Ellerby felt he knew it all already. He learned a bit more after he said our precious cutlery had gone over the side with the washing-up water. We managed to share the remains, and Leo's Boy Scout knife, fork and spoon set, until the ship reached port.

When we were a few days out from Loch Ewe, I was going along the alleyway balancing kits of food from the galley when the blackout curtain on the second cook's door parted. 'Look sahib, me sick.' He pulled his lungi aside, and I was almost sick as well. In the short distance to the cabin, my appetite disappeared. I told the boys that the second cook was sick. 'I know,' said Leo. 'He's got a dose. He also showed it to me. I hope he didn't touch the grub. Anyway, Ben, if you don't want yours I'll have it'.

To save time and cost in port discharging the ballast, the mate told us to take turns down the holds, filling skips and dumping the contents over the side. The Old Man volunteered to pay each of us sixpence an hour, with a reminder that it was a gratuitous payment as we weren't entitled to overtime. The job would have been mandatory anyway, so we jumped at the chance.

By then the ship was out of convoy and just a couple of days from port. The weather was fine and we would earn enough for one or two good nights ashore, depending on southern hospitality.

We docked in Baltimore on 11 April, three weeks after leaving Loch Ewe. Ellery was told to go ashore as soon as possible to bring back cutlery of any kind, and not to return without it. We were sure he was just the right person for such a mission, and it would teach him to be more careful in future.

Ten days in Baltimore, a fine port and a great town for sailors, helped us forget about the war. The Americans hadn't quite got used to it, although they had started a building programme for merchant ships which surpassed anything in maritime history. I looked across the harbour at one being launched from Bethlehem steel shipyard and didn't realise that it was one of the early Liberty ships, of which 2,708 would be completed in US yards between 1941 and 1945. The average cost per ship was 1.8 million dollars and average time to build would be 39 days. Bethlehem built the first, with 383 others to follow.

When the ship started loading military equipment, we knew that the short trip back to the UK wasn't on, and that it looked like the Middle East again. It would be a long passage of 6,500 miles to the Cape, and another 5,500 or so to Suez or the Persian Gulf. The Renfrew had already steamed more than 35,000 miles since TR took command in Cardiff the previous July. It was clear that this was going to be a much longer trip than the first one.

There was nothing lacking in the hospitality boys in uniform received ashore in the USA. We had advice from dockers, and others servicing the ship, on where to go and what to do in Baltimore; none of it was sightseeing, but it was all affordable. An invitation from the ladies of Baltimore to attend a large gala dance in aid of some War Relief Fund was accepted by Leo and me. The other two couldn't dance. There was no charge for anyone in uniform and there were plenty of us there. Food and drinks were free and all the dances seemed to be ladies' choice. There was no chance of a disruptive air raid warning, and it turned out to be a long night which passed too quickly.

Leo had his mind set on a gramophone to liven up the cabin. He danced with a mature well-dressed lady who offered to supply one. Her husband was a top reporter with the *Baltimore Sun* and worked every evening and through the night producing the morning paper. She apologised, he didn't have time to deliver the gramophone to the ship, so Leo agree to go home with her to make sure it was suitable. It required another couple of night inspections, with some operating tuition thrown in, before Leo took delivery of the gramophone. The lady even gave him a full tin of gramophone needles, records of Gracie Fields singing 'Sally' and Clyde McCoy playing 'Sugar Blues' on his trumpet.

My partner was different to Leo's; she just liked dancing with sailors and was a mine of information about the USA, and Baltimore in particular. I learned a lot without asking and she knew where to go for the best results. As we were dancing to a famous orchestra, Guy Lombardo and his Royal Canadians, playing what she called 'the sweetest music this side of heaven', she asked me whether I wanted his autograph. Before I could answer, she tore a piece off someone else's programme and brought it back signed 'Best wishes to Ben, from Guy Lombardo'. She wanted to know where we were going the following evening, and I suggested a burlesque show downtown. She said that women were not welcome in burlesques, and I told her I knew that. She was quick on the uptake and I never saw her again.

The mate gave us one night off together and we visited as many entertainment venues as possible before arriving at the Silver Dollar, a well known up-market nightclub in Downtown Baltimore. Even with the generous rate of exchange at more than four dollars to a pound agreed with America for the duration of the War, 25 cents for a small beer was a bit much. In the other places we had been, the same thing was only 10 cents. We were told that when customers left the club, they were given a new silver dollar. Unfortunately, it didn't apply to those who were asked to leave.

The Gaiety Theatre was similar to the Glasgow Empire. They both had front and back stalls and balconies, but that is where the similarity ended. It was our first burlesque show and we wanted the best view: from the front seats in the balcony. A girl, wearing a tray round her neck and little else, kept shouting, 'Get your telescopes and popcorn now before the show starts.' Telescopes cost 25 cents and popcorn 5 cents. We didn't want popcorn and didn't need telescopes as we all had good eyesight.

We were all keen to go to a burlesque show in Baltimore and see why they were to be banned that year in New York. Topless chorus girls at the Windmill in London and the Folies Bergères in Paris weren't allowed to move during their act, but at the Gaiety there were no restrictions. Some members of the audience brought their own telescopes. The dirty jokes told by inter-round comedians may be acceptable in the 1990s, but not in the 1940s. Parts of the show were over the top, so to speak, even to broad-minded ships' apprentices. We didn't go back to the Gaiety, and couldn't go back to the Silver Dollar.

Ten days in Baltimore wasn't long enough. The hospitality lived up to everything we had heard about southern ports, although Baltimore was only just below the Mason-Dixon line.

The ship left on 21 April, fully loaded with cargo stores and bunkers at a good sailing draft of 23 feet. The long, 6,500 mile haul down to the Cape would take at least a month, and many critical decisions would be made by TR during that passage. Good weather was expected all the way to Cape Town, but that must have been his least concern. Direct courses from Chesapeake Bay to the Cape passed close to St. Paul's Rocks. This isolated, uninhabited mass, rising up from the ocean bed, was the cause of many sailing ship losses. The rocks were situated a few miles north of the Equator, and about 500 miles east of South America. Naval authorities in Baltimore had advised the Old Man to give them a wide berth. German surface raiders were sinking ships in that part of the Atlantic and U-boats were being deployed there to deal with the increasing number of vessels carrying cargoes from the States to the Middle East. No support of any kind was available, and ships sailed independently.

The ship had crossed the Equator twice since Leo and I joined. The 2nd. Mate decided it was time we were introduced to Father Neptune. He said it was overdue, so a large tarpaulin was rigged between the derricks on number 3 hatch and filled with water. We were liberally covered with foul-smelling soogie used for washing paint and cleaning decks, and Alec Livingstone had the satisfaction of chucking us into the salt water one by one for a good scrub down with a long handle broom. It just made grimy apprentices more grimy, The 2nd. Mate was about 6½ feet tall, with the biggest hands I ever saw. He issued the Father Neptune certificates and made us clean up the mess.

The ship was two weeks out of Baltimore and we hadn't seen or heard another vessel. One of the two fresh water tanks ran out and Chippy found he couldn't get down number 4 hatch to switch over to the other one. A large crate containing aircraft sections had been loaded on top of the hatch and blocked access to the ladder. One of the double-bottom tanks had been filled with boiler water, but when they pumped that up it tasted salty. The tank hadn't been flushed out after a previous ballasting. It was a disaster to be on the Equator, two weeks away from port, with no fresh drinking water.

Boiled up in tea, the DB water was terrible, but coffee was drinkable. It was coffee or cocoa for everyone until bunker coal in the fore end of the 'tween deck was either used or moved to access the tank. It wasn't *really* everyone; there were five exceptions, the apprentices and the 2nd Mate. We found that an enamel liferaft dipper, tied to the end of a length of boat lacing, was narrow enough to go down the sounding pipe of the inaccessible fresh water tank. Each night on the middle watch one of us filled an empty seven pound pickle jar. The 2nd Mate was, without question, happy to have a decent cup of tea twice daily.

One week before we left Baltimore, Bill the Newfoundland gunner was taken off the ship by the naval authorities. Gunners all signed on articles as deckhands and were moved around from one ship to another without warning. On this occasion they were probably short of gunners on a UK bound convoy. We were all sorry to lose Bill; he was a solid old Newffie, a fine shipmate and if it had come to lifeboat drill, he would have been a good man in a boat.

There was plenty of gunnery practice between Baltimore and Cape Town and by then we got to know the armament thoroughly and how to get the best out of it. We also knew how antiquated it all was and realised that the title 'Defensively Equipped Merchant Ships' (DEMS) was more a morale booster than a reality. Our luck held and the ship anchored in Table Bay on 24 May. From then until we sailed again on the 30th, there was a spate of sickness, ranging from suspected heart attack to heat exhaustion and other ailments. The shore doctor was busy every day the ship was in port.

By the time the war started, our 1st. Mate had retired from the sea. He was in his mid-sixties and now he had voluntarily returned. I respected him for it. There were many who packed it in and went ashore to work. Considering the dreadful sailing conditions then on most British merchant ships, who could blame them? For the majority of men who had followed the sea all their lives, it was a case of just carrying on and hoping the war would go away soon. For youngsters like me, it was an exciting, exhilarating, toughening-up process, without which there was no way up the ladder. I realised this early on and worked hard towards a successful career. Although I liked some more than others, I respected every senior officer of every ship on which I sailed. Captain T. R. Reid could have been classed a role model. Everything he did was by the book, although some said he wrote it himself and that there was no room for argument.

From Cape Town the ship was bound direct to Basra in the Persian Gulf, a distance of about 5,500 miles. There was submarine activity around the Cape and we were warned that armed German or Japanese surface raiders were operating on the trade routes to the Red Sea and the Gulf. The Old Man ordered full gunnery watches 24 hours a day.

Eight days after we left Cape Town, the Elysia, a fine Anchor Line ship, overhauled us, making good time. We had been in Cape Town together, but he would arrive in the Gulf well before us. Our old mate was excited; he was one of the pre-war masters of the ship and had been on board before sailing. He wouldn't see her again. Sparks picked up a lifeboat transmitter message saying that Elysia had been sunk right ahead of us by a raider and warned us to look out for boats.

The ship carried on the same course until daybreak, when the masts and funnel of a large unidentifiable vessel appeared on the horizon. The first time a cargo ship saw an armed raider was usually the last. TR's 90 degree alteration to port, and his demand for every bit of speed the *Renfrew* was capable of, had a startling effect. The old ship shuddered objectionably at having to exceed her top speed of 10 knots. The masts and funnel of the other vessel didn't dip over the horizon quickly enough and the African coast couldn't show up soon enough.

We sighted land the following morning. It was 10 June and I had forgotten my birthday on the eighth. Leo suggested telling the cook so he could make tabnabs (currant buns) for us, but he didn't think it necessary to let the cook know the birthday was two days earlier. Ten days later, we entered the Persian Gulf, and four days after that berthed at Basra. The steaming time from Baltimore to Basra was two months.

CHAPTER 5   Distressed British Seaman

The ship arrived Basra at 1.20 p.m. on 24 June. Sailing up the Persian Gulf was hot. The close confines of the Shatt El Arab were hotter, but when we tied up alongside the berth it was almost unbearable. Our windchutes, made from empty 14lb. jam tins sticking out of the cabin portholes, only attracted sand, smells and swarms of large flying insects we never knew existed. Working on deck in the Red Sea and Suez Canal was comfortable, by comparison.

The ship started discharging at six o'clock in the evening; even the Arabs couldn't work in the afternoon. The chief engineer was taken ashore to hospital the following day, suffering from heat exhaustion, and stayed there for 14 days. Temperatures in the shade often reached 120 degrees. It was almost impossible to walk on the steel decks during the day. Frying eggs on them was more than a possibility.

The Port of Basra, then, consisted of one very long quay. The *Renfrew* was berthed as far as it was possible to be from the dock entrance. Only dockers and those directly involved with business on board the ship were allowed through the gates. With no refrigerators of any kind on the *Renfrew*, large blocks of ice were delivered each day. Men carried them on their backs all the way from the dock gates. This was during the hottest part of the day, when cargo wasn't being worked. The size of the blocks had diminished considerably by the time the cook checked them into the ice box.

Ship's clusters provided illumination for the hatches and helped to increase the swarms of large flying creatures attracted by the lights. They were more friendly to the Arabs than to us.

After 21 days in Basra, discharging a full cargo with ship's gear, we were pleased to leave the place, even though it was only down-river to Abadan.

The long time in Basra took its toll. In 120+ degrees and no cold drinks apart from a few beers ashore, in premises devoid of hygiene, where cold food had to be eaten hot, I succumbed to a severe attack of dysentery and was removed to hospital. Water melons were one of the few luxuries readily available in Basra, and in the absence of anything else, we made the most of them. When they were diagnosed as the cause of the dysentery, I never ate another.

Compared to living conditions on the ship, and particularly during the previous three weeks, the BP hospital in Abadan was idyllic. Temperatures were maintained at about 65 degrees, the beds were comfortable, and the food *seemed* superb. Waking in the morning with lovely Persian nurses smilingly taking my pulse, was the cause of memorable moments for some time afterwards. The nurses were not only stunning, but extremely considerate. They kept us informed about the doctors' movements around the wards and, when all was clear, we smoked. A pound from the Renfrew pay-off of nine pounds and ten shillings paid my share of cold beer, smuggled in by the nurses just before lights-out.

After five wonderful days, a doctor told me that I would be leaving hospital the following evening. I told him I wasn't well enough to go and he replied with a smile, 'They all feel like that after our treatment.' I was put up by BP in their residential home and classed as a DBS (Distressed British Seaman). The few days there were really enjoyable, but sadly terminated by the British Consul, who found me a ship. It was bound for India, which he understood was the general direction taken by the *Renfrew*. I would be landed there and conveyed, some way or other, to my own ship, if possible. I thanked him for the precise instructions and joined another tramp steamer as DBS.

It was exactly 12 months since we had first sailed from Greenock. Much had happened since then. A full 620 British ships, totalling 2½ million tons, had been sunk. The war at sea, which had started the day it was declared with the tragic sinking of Athenia, was not improving. On board *Renfrew*, we knew little about these events. Communications between tramp ships and the outside world were limited. Rumours circulating ashore among other seamen were generally the best sources of information available. Wireless telegraphy, earphones and morse key were attended by a radio operator 24 hours a day at sea, but transmitting could only be done in emergencies. Strict radio silence was always

Convoy PQ 18 – the biggest Allied convoy to Russia – under attack from enemy torpedo planes and U-boats. The photograph shows a near miss on HMS *Ashanti* with HMS *Eskimo* in foreground, September 1942.

observed, whether in convoy or sailing independently. Merchant seamen had a responsibility to keep their mouths shut when ashore; ports in neutral countries were well stocked with enemy agents and their local satellites. The saying that most seamen, when they got ashore, never passed the first pub up the street was true enough. Posters in every city and town in the UK advising 'Walls Have Ears' and 'Careless Talk Cost Lives' had to be remembered even more so abroad.

The Stanhope Steamship vessel I joined as DBS was an Empire boat. We called them 'ninety-day wonders', built very quickly in the UK to outlast the War. She had a Liverpool crew with a Glasgow master and chief steward who lived next door to one another in the Queen's Park area of the city. According to the disgruntled engineers on the ship, this close association had a derogatory effect on their living standards. It was my first white crew ship and an opportunity to compare it with the Indians.

As a DBS, I did not have to work while on board the ship. I accepted this satisfactory situation and welcomed being a passenger, with the use of the hospital on the top deck and £8 of the Renfrew pay-off still intact.

The vessel left Abadan and anchored off Bandar Abbas, at the entrance to the Gulf, to discharge some cargo. It was similar to what the Renfrew unloaded at Basra, consisting of military stores and crated aircraft. The valuable cargo was lowered by derrick into Arab dhows lashed together. The size and weight of one of the large aircraft containers was too much for the dhows, which were cut adrift from one another, allowing the aircraft to sink slowly down into the deep waters of the Persian Gulf.

The 600 miles or so from Bandar Abbas to Karachi, then in India, was considered relatively safe for British ships. I had the hospital to myself and ate in the engineers' messroom. This was an improvement on the last 12 months sharing a similar size cabin with three others and sitting on a settee or lower bunk, balancing a food container on my lap. Unfortunately, the grub was no better and the cooking worse. It didn't matter to me, but it did to the engineers. They had been away from home for several months long enough on a long voyage, when the novelty of close confinement with others was wearing off. Nothing the cook could produce satisfied the engineers. Before he put it on the table one of them would say, 'what kind of s—- have you made today?', or words to that effect. Unfortunately for the engineers, the cook was a former New Zealand Army physical training instructor. I became friendly with him. It always paid on a tramp ship to keep on the right side of the cook. We berthed alongside at Karachi and arrangements got underway to get me to Calcutta to rejoin the Renfrew, due there some time. Many of the crew were overdrawn and the captain wouldn't advance them money to go ashore. My £8 excited their interest, and my popularity had seldom been greater.

The port of Karachi wasn't exactly a sailor's paradise, and not a place to jump ship, whatever the conditions on board. Seamen could never be considered tourists. One trip around Karachi in a ghari for a few annas was usually enough for a first tripper. Others never bothered and looked for the nearest place to drink. The bosun and one of the deck crew assured me that it was even worse than Bombay, so the three of us found refuge in a mission-type building which sold liquor. My Renfrew pay-off was soon in action. It was pleasing to be able to contribute something. The drinks were cheap, but all they sold were large bottles of Guinness. I had never tasted it and didn't like the look of it. My mates assured me that the taste was an acquired one and took some time to appreciate. I didn't remember getting back to the ship. The hospital door opened on to the maindeck beside number 4 hatch. I came to with someone standing beside the bed and asked whether he was the laundry man. He scooped up all the clothes lying on the deck and was never seen again. Go-ashore gear was then in short supply.

Arrangements were progressing to get me back to the Renfrew. After two more nights ashore, the Old Man said I would be going by train from Karachi to Calcutta, which would only take three or four days. The cook was also strapped for cash and asked for a loan of ten shillings. He assured me that if I ever went to New Plymouth, in New Zealand, his wife would refund it. After one night ashore, the cook returned on board with a satisfied look. Two of the engineers came back the worse for wear.

The ship's agent took me by ghari to Karachi railway station with the old leather suitcase and a white duck canvas kitbag I made on the Renfrew. Like everywhere else, the station was a heaving mass of humanity.

Baron Renfrew, 1935-1973. Built by D. & W. Henderson, Glasgow; sold to Greek owners 1961, and scrapped in Turkey, 1973.

(Post-war picture taken by Skyfotos)

CERTIFICATE OF DISCHARGE

Dis. 1.

FOR A SEAMAN DISCHARGED BEFORE A SUPERINTENDENT OR A CONSULAR OFFICER.

ISSUED BY THE MINISTRY OF SHIPPING. No. **41**

Name of Ship and Official Number, Port of Registry and Gross Tonnage.	Horse Power.	Description of Voyage or Employment.
S. S. *Baron Renfrew* Ardrossan 163841 G.T. 3635	324	Foreign

Name of Seaman.	Year of Birth.	Place of Birth.
George. S. Gunn	1923	Glasgow

Rank or Rating.	No. of R.N.R. Commission or Certif.	No. of Cert. (if any).
Apprentice	—	—

Date of Engagement.	Place of Engagement.	Copy of Report of Character.*	
26. 2. 42	Hull	For Ability.	For General Conduct.

Date of Discharge.	Place of Discharge.	VG	VG
16. 4. 42	Abadan		

I **certify** that the above particulars are correct and that the above named Seaman was discharged accordingly.

Dated this 16ᵗʰ day of July 1942

Thos. T. Reid ....MASTER.

AUTHENTICATED BY .... Signature of Superintendent or Consular Officer

* If the Seaman does not require a Certificate of his character, enter "Endorsement not required." in the spaces provided for the copy of the Report.

Signature of Seaman .......G.S. Gunn.....

NOTE.—Any person who forges or fraudulently alters any Certificate or Report, or copy of a Report, or who makes use of any Certificate or Report, or copy of a Report, which is forged or altered or does not belong to him, shall for each such offence be deemed guilty of a misdemeanour, and may be fined or imprisoned.

N.B.—Should this Certificate come into the possession of any person to whom it does not belong, it should be handed to the Superintendent of the nearest Mercantile Marine Office, or be transmitted to the Registrar-General of Shipping and Seamen, Tower Hill, London, E.C.3.

Certificate of discharge at Abadan.

Without the agent it would have been almost impossible to get to the ticket office window. I did my best to shield him from the mob while he made the reservation. There was heated conversation between him and the booking clerk before the tickets were issued. I wanted to know the problem. He mumbled something about political trouble. The clerk intervened and said, 'The British have put Mr. Ghandi in jail, the people are ripping up the railway lines and the train could only get as far as Allahabad, about 500 miles from Calcutta.' I knew the captain of the Stanhope wanted rid of me, but I had hoped that it would not be like that. Clearly, so did the ship's agent, so I told him to get me a ghari back to the docks and not to bother coming along.

The hospital was still available and all hands were ashore. I soon caught up with them, now using their own rupees for the Guinness. My two mates were in the company of a couple of Americans from a Liberty ship. The opinion was, I would never get back to the *Renfrew*, even if she made it to Calcutta. I didn't like the prospect of going any further on this ship as a DBS. The Yanks were short of a utility man on the Liberty and there would be no problem getting the job. She was a new ship, the food and conditions were much better than most of our tramps, and a seaman's money was as good as a British 2nd Mate's.

A utility man did the odd jobs around the ship as part of the deck crew. It would only be a temporary position as two of the deckhands were skinning out when the ship got to a decent port. I agreed to take the job and they would confirm it with the master. When I turned up for breakfast the following morning, the Old Man wasn't pleased to see that I was still around. After explaining what had happened to Mr. Ghandi and the railway lines, I told him about the job on the Liberty. This didn't please him either and he reminded me of his responsibilities.

There was no chance of getting overland to Calcutta. The American consul gave his blessing for a move to the Liberty, but the British consul interfered and arrangements were made for a flight from Karachi across India.

Unfortunately, there was limited baggage allowance on the RAF flying boat so my old leather suitcase, packed with effects, had to be left on board. The steward promised it would be sent on to Glasgow eventually. It never happened. All flights then were for military purposes only. This one was taking army, navy and RAF top brass to Calcutta in preparation for invasion by the Japanese, who had recently captured Singapore, conquered Burma, and sunk the battleships *Prince of Wales* and *Repulse* in the Pacific. In the few months since Pearl Harbour any doubts about the Japanese resolve to include India in their Far East conquests were expelled.

Having lost my number ones to the bogus laundry man in Karachi, I felt inadequate among all the gold braid and insignia on board the plane. The well-worn white shirt, flannel trousers and khaki topee were rather prominent. The contents of the duck canvas kitbag would have to be supplemented in Calcutta, subject to a small cash advance from the captain. Cotton tropical gear was cheap in India.

This was my first flight. We took off from an inlet near Karachi and landed a couple of times on the way to refuel. From the air, the landing areas looked like small ponds. There was nothing to eat because all unnecessary weight had been removed, including the interior panelling. Drinks and snacks were available during the fuel-stops. When it got round that I was a Distressed British Seaman, my fellow passengers were most considerate and sympathetic. It was a good flight and my last in a flying boat.

The aircraft landed on the Hooghly river in Calcutta. Passengers were ferried ashore and I understood, the dispersal point was Grant's Hotel in the centre of the city. It sounded modest enough. The outside of the hotel was well protected with sandbags, which also obscured the name. Inside, the opulence and splendour were immediately apparent. It was *the* Grand Hotel. Just right for my fellow passengers, but not for a tramp ship apprentice down to his last rupee and a half. There was no time to change my mind, as I was quickly relieved of the kitbag by a turbaned bellboy and led to the reception desk. I then followed him across the floor of the Palm Court, dressed in the same short-sleeve shirt, a more crumpled than ever pair of trousers, and the khaki topee still in place. The bellboy carried the kitbag in traditional seaman's style, over his shoulder.

Residents and their memsahibs, languorously reclining, listening to the muted orchestra music, and accompanied by a large number of high ranking military officers, also watching this small procession, must have wondered where it came from. Looking at them there, I could see the Grand Hotel was well protected inside as well as outside.

I had never before been in such an hotel. Nobody seemed to want money, even the bellboy. At the time, I wondered why. I was starving and certainly couldn't eat there. Forgetting about the recent dysentery, for half a rupee I bought a large mutton curry with rice and beer. This left one rupee for a ghari to the ship agents in the morning. The pleading cries of 'backsheesh, no mama, no papa, sahib' as I wondered around the streets of Calcutta that evening had to be ignored. The poverty and deprivation was pitiful to see and even worse than other ports I had been to in India.

Captain T. R. Reid was genuinely pleased to see me in McKinnon Mackenzie's office at nine the following morning. He said there had been several cases of sickness since Basra, mainly sandfly fever heat exhaustion and suspected malaria. In my absence, the apprentices worked watch and watch (four hours on and four hours off) spending six hours each at the wheel and six hours working on deck each day at sea. The 1st Mate was in hospital in Calcutta. One of the khalassis dropped a large, steel anchor shackle on his foot and it had turned gangrenous. He wouldn't be sailing, and TR would keep a watch at sea himself.

With the very strong current in the river Hooghly, ships were moored to buoys by anchor cable at each end. One 90 foot length of cable was dragged all the way along the deck from forward to aft then back again, when the ship left the buoys. It was then that the old mate was injured, but it was hoped that he would rejoin the ship at a discharge port, wherever that happened to be. Alternatively, he would be sent home on another ship as DBS.

The captain and agent's runner took me to the shipping office while they signed on a new Lascar crew. We were mobbed by a heaving mass, all waving papers and certificates and shouting, 'Me Clan Line, me P&O, me Baron Line. I sail with you before'. There was no shortage of Indians wanting to go back to sea despite the dangerous occupation it had become. They knew about that, but still competed for selection.

A serang and tindal, who had previously sailed on one of the company's ships, were signed on first and they chose the other 33. Their papers were checked, they were all medically examined, innoculated against smallpox and signed on to report on board by 7.00 a.m. the following day, 28 August 1942.

Despite the palatial room in the Grand, I was glad to get back to the cramped cabin on board the *Renfrew*.

Kiddipor Dock in Calcutta was a hive of activity. The saying at sea that a port was so busy you could walk across the ships seemed literally true. I was given the plum job of cleaning the brass on the ship's bridge just before sailing. The 2nd mate, who had been promoted, was considerably giving me an easy time for a few days. I had recovered from the dysentery to the extent that I was able to eat the Renfrew food with little revulsion.

The scene from up top was of a mass of white-clad humanity swarming over ships' decks and hatches, discharging or loading the contents. A couple of minutes after the air raid warning siren sounded, there was not a soul to be seen. The 3rd mate, working up on monkey island (navigating bridge), tripped over a lanyard for the PAC rocket ejector, which went off with a loud bang. Although it was a beautiful, cloudless day with not a Jap to be seen, ships started firing into the air, which encouraged others to do so as well. The all clear sounded and the white sea gradually re-formed, but not as quickly as it had disappeared. I had seen air raid warnings in the UK, but they never generated the same reaction as they had in Calcutta.

The more I saw the conditions ashore, the more understandable I found the desire of so many to sign on ships. In 1943, over 750,000 died of famine in the province of Bengal. Unknowingly, we were seeing at first hand the beginning of the end of the British Raj in India,and without any Japanese intervention. By 1947 it would all be over.

Although India was a fascinating country, we were pleased to get out of it and back to sea. There was speculation about our next port of call. Being an old hand at war games, T.R. divulged nothing. Although he knew where we were bound, nobody else would until he opened his sealed orders. Australia looked the best bet. It was reassuring to be told in Calcutta by some armchair sailors, there were only about 30 German and Japanese submarines operating in the Indian Ocean.

The 3,500-mile passage from Calcutta took just over three weeks. The long trip in warm weather took its toll on the ice-box and for a time before we arrived in port there was no fresh food. Large barrels of salt meat and seven-pound tins of bully beef were sustaining enough, and almost conformed to alternatives in the scale of provisions included in the Articles of Agreement. One thing we all missed more than anything else was a cold glass of milk. The apprentices' monthly 'whack' of dry stores contained three tins each of Nestlé's Condensed Milk. This was used on porridge, puddings and in tea and cocoa. Only one tin at a time was issued. Two quarter-inch holes were made in the top of the tins opposite one another and sealed with small wooden plugs. By blowing one end, the milk was served from the other. When the tin was not in use, the wooden plugs were kept in to keep the cockroaches out. We each had our own tin in use at any one time.

The passage from Calcutta to Fremantle was 23 days. Although the ship was only there for 24 hours, the gunners said it was three and a half months since we'd been to a civilised place and they intended to make the most of it. They did, and by the time I got ashore there was an international dust-up taking place between Fred and his crew, and some Aussies in the main street of Fremantle. It was like a scene from a Wild West movie. Fremantle in 1942, with its dusty streets and ramshackle buildings, was a perfect setting.

My intervention was ill-timed and I was reported to the mate for fighting in the streets. Alec Livingstone was a reasonable officer; he accepted I was only trying to stop the fight. Fred said they were defending Nelson's honour, as one of the Aussie sailors had pulled at his collar and made disparaging remarks about His Majesty's Navy.

Perth was a fine city and we got a much better welcome there than from the Australian Navy at Fremantle. The mate said that my activities ashore in the morning hadn't been reported to T.R. and that I could have the night off, as long as I stayed out of trouble. We caught a bus from Fremantle to Perth, started off in a dance-hall and stayed there for the rest of the evening. It looked as though a major hen party was taking place; the hall was full of girls without partners. Either Australian men didn't dance, or they were all on their way to war in the Middle East.

As Leo related later to our attentive shipmates, 'we were snaffled up by a bevy of beauties as soon as we entered the hall; they were brandishing cloakroom tickets which paid for our drinks all night. It's a pity you two can't dance.' When I asked about the Aussie men, one girl said, 'Our guys are too rough to enjoy dancing, not like you boys from home. Anyway we like your uniforms better.'

The ship was due to dock at Melbourne and Sydney to discharge the cargo, then load coal at Newcastle in New South Wales. The mate said it didn't matter whether we went east or west from there, it was bound to be in the general direction of home.

After Leo's and my one-night-stand in Perth, we all looked forward hopefully to long discharge and loading periods in the other Australian ports.

Aerial view of Fremantle Harbour

CHAPTER 6 From Sunny Australia back to the Cold North

The ship left Fremantle on 17 September and arrived at Melbourne two days later. With a fresh wind, rough sea and heavy swell on the beam, she had a good roll on her all the way across the Great Australian Bight. The cook had problems preparing the food, the stewards in the dining room serving it, and everyone had a problem eating it. We were glad to get alongside the quay at Melbourne. Unfortunately, the agent in Fremantle told T.R. about the fracas ashore and the Mate was instructed to have a word with us. On board, the ship gunners were under the authority of the master, but ashore they were answerable to the naval authorities. The mate had to make an example of someone – and I was the only person available. He kept me on board during the first two days in port, then remembered he wanted a new trilby and couldn't get off the ship in time to buy one.

With the money, the hat size, and advice to keep out of the way of the gunners, I went ashore, ran into four of them and was coaxed into a pub for a drink. The barman wouldn't serve me, said I looked under age and asked me to leave. Fred told him what he thought of Australia and they had to leave as well. Licensed premises in Melbourne closed at 6 o'clock, so did shops which sold hats. It was no good going back to the ship without the hat and, as I was in the cart anyway, I stayed with the others and ended up in a licensed restaurant. It was a night to remember. Fred ordered a bottle of wine, but there was a problem. The manageress said that wine could only be served with a meal. An arguement broke out. Fred was convinced that he was being unfairly treated; the manageress was sure that Fred and his party were drunk. The police were called and took them away for a couple of hours, cooling off in the local gaol. Someone would have to go there to vouch for them. I promised to do it and passed the time at the Ice Rink. When I found the gaol they had been released. Back aboard ,the ship I was told the Mate had gone ashore 'without a hat'.

The last thing I expected to find in a city like Melbourne was an ice rink. I had learned to skate at Crossmyloof rink in Glasgow just before the War. For a shilling on Friday evenings, we saw an ice hockey match,

followed by a couple of hours, general skating. Games between the two Glasgow teams, Mohawks and Kelvingrove, were contested as ferociously as football matches between Rangers and Celtic, but much more spectacularly. Bingham's boating pond on Great Western Road provided free skating in the winter. An ice rink seemed out of place in warm sunny Melbourne.

Archie, the 4th Engineer, was as schooner-rigged as the rest of us. The Chief gave him an afternoon off to buy a pair of shoes, as his others were only suitable for the engine room and stokehold. Unfortunately, I took the same size; he borrowed them promising to be back by six and didn't return until eight, whereupon he immediately flaked out on the settee, wearing his own new shoes. My date at the ice rink was gone, and so were my only pair of go-ashore shoes. When Archie came to, he couldn't remember which pubs he had visited and where he had left the parcel.

Five days in Melbourne, discharging half the cargo, was followed by a week in Sydney, leisurely unloading the rest. Sydney was a very different place to quiet sedate Melbourne. It was big, boisterous and fast becoming Americanized. Sydney Harbour was a breathtaking sight and the 3rd Mate said it could accommodate all the world's navies at anchor at the same time. Sydney was also the first place in Australia where I saw, heard and read the slogan, 'Keep Australia White'. This clearly couldn't include the indigenous population, and there was exception for a limited number of Chinese. Some cynics said it was for laundry purposes only.

We saw as much of Sydney as possible in one week. A visit to Taronga Park Zoo, built on its own island in the harbour, was a must, the King's Cross area, with it's expanding gay and lesbian activities was best avoided, even in 1942. It was no place for sailors and I doubt whether many went there. Their limited time ashore was usually devoted to more seamanlike pursuits.

Ellerby, the apprentice from London, found Sydney very much to his liking. He was adopted by a girl and her family and failed to turn up in time to sail for Newcastle. When we arrived there, he was on the quay to meet the ship. T.R. wasn't amused, logged him and stopped any further shore leave in Australia. Ellerby decided to jump ship, packed all his gear and asked Leo and me to help him get it over the dockyard fence. During the night before sailing, at a pre-arranged point, we chucked it over and off he went in a car with his new family. We never saw him again and he was logged as a deserter.

Before the ship sailed the following morning, Australian immigration officials interrogated us. We gave them a photograph of someone we didn't know and they went ashore satisfied but smiling.

It was not surprising to hear some years later of Ellerby's successful career in the Australian Merchant Service.

Newcastle NSW was a complete contrast to Melbourne and Sydney. It was an underdeveloped industrial port, specialising in the production and export of coal. The ship arrived in a light condition ready to load a full cargo for South America. Loading the coal would take four or five days and we felt it would be long enough in a place like that. It was a very wrong assumption. The residents of Newcastle couldn't have been nicer or more hospitable and it was a great place to go ashore.

The old mate rejoined the ship in Sydney after a trip as DBS from Calcutta to Fremantle, then a long uncomfortable 2,000 mile haul by train across the full expanse of Australia and the Great Victoria Desert. Having lost a big toe and being in his mid sixties, he wasn't in the best physical condition by the time he arrived on board. After an absence of almost two months, he signed on Articles again and his monthly wage of £22.10.6 and home allotment of £10 recommenced. The mates resumed their original ranks.

Loading coal in Australia was no different to doing it in South Africa or the UK: it got everywhere. All portholes and doors were kept closed, and because it was very warm at the time, the cabins and other compartments were like sweat-boxes. Apart from sweeping up, uncovering and covering the hatches, ensuring the cargo was well trimmed into the wings of the holds, there was little deck work to do. The long passage across the Pacific Ocean from Australia to South America would allow enough time and good weather to catch up with everything.

Although there was no shore leave during the day, every night was free and we made the best of them. I sought out the nearest dance hall and got the same reception as I had in Perth. A large Aussie naval vessel was also in port and on this occasion there was a lot of uniformed competition. That's when I met Brenda. She was about three inches taller than me, a beautiful girl and a wonderful dancer. She didn't seem to mind the difference in height and nor did I.

Unfortunately, an Australian sailor also fancied her and cut in when he wasn't wanted. We had a few strong words, which could have gone further if I hadn't decided to go to the gents. In there, I was recommended to cool it as the sailor was lightweight boxing champion of South Australia and their ship had just returned from working off the west coast of the USA. During that time he had had a number of fights and won them all. The ship's company was very proud of him. I immediately went back into the hall, apologised and introduced him to Brenda. He then pushed off.

With only two more nights to go, our time in Newcastle seemed short, not only for me but for Archie. After one night ashore, he was full of praise for pubs that never close and pork-roast suppers. He recommended one place in particular and asked me to join him the following evening.

Brenda had other ideas and after another evening at the dance hall, I was asked home to meet the folks and couldn't resist an invitation to stay the night. Apprentices were supposed to be back on board the ship by midnight, but with that mate it was alright as long as he saw us around at six in the morning.

Brenda's father, Fred, had spent most of the First War in Britain and turned what was meant to be a romantic evening into a nostalgic one. After many months in a ship's bunk, and all the time at sea sleeping with a lifejacket under my head, Brenda's soft receptive bed and large scented feather pillow into which my body sunk in to complete oblivion, was heavenly.

Brenda slept in another room, woke me at five with tea and toast and tearfully kissed me goodbye. I fell in love with Brenda, and every day for the next month before we arrived in Montevideo, I wrote one paragraph of a long letter to her. There was no mail service between Uruguay and Australia, the letter was never posted and my thoughts about Brenda became just pleasant memories.

George Gunn and shipmates in Montevideo, 1942.
(Gordon, Chippy and Fred from Battersea).

The ship left Newcastle on the 20 October for her longest passage of the voyage: right across the Pacific Ocean, around Cape Horn and up the east coast of South America to Montevideo. She arrived there on the 24 November, a distance of more than 9,000 miles.

Nine thousand miles seemed a long way to take a cargo of coal in the middle of a war. Decisions on where the ship went were entirely in the hands of the Ministry of War Transport. How they did it was up to the master. Normally, this passage would have been through the Magellan Straits to ensure the best weather by avoiding Cape Horn. TR had been warned of submarine activity at the Straits and decided to go round the Horn. As he said, 'I've never been round there. It's a good opportunity to do so and at the same time keep out of the way of the Japs. There are few worse places in the world to get into trouble than God-forsaken Tierra Del Fuego. I understand the inhabitants still have cannibal tendencies.'

Coal is not as benign a cargo to carry on a ship as may be expected. Properly controlled ventilation is essential to prevent internal combustion and fire in the holds. As the wind changed and our courses altered the large cowls on the cargo hold ventilators had to be turned in a favourable direction. During night watches the standby man did this on his own. Balancing on top of the mast tables with the ship rolling violently and trying to coax them round sufficiently to satisfy the officer of the watch, wasn't my favourite job. Ellerby's departure put us back to four hours on four hours off with dog watches. Two apprentices and the two Indian quartermasters did all the bridge watches and steering, with the other apprentice on day work.

We took advantage of the long haul across the Pacific and the good weather, to get the ship in the best possible condition for arrival in the UK. For camouflage purposes, all British ships were painted admiralty grey. They all had the same neglected look and it was difficult for officers and crews to generate the pride and interest they had had in their ships before the war. Maintenance and some improvements could be carried out on long voyages out east, but continually ploughing back and forward across the Atlantic in convoy made that impossible.

Apart from the Straits of Magellan, it was unlikely there would be any submarine or surface raider problems in this part of the Pacific, but the Old Man insisted on so many four-inch practices that every member of the gun's crew could change rounds automatically under any conditions. Alec Livingstone, our 2nd mate and Gunnery Officer, was accurate with the range-finder and we didn't always miss the target.

Although the ship was stored in Australia for a long passage, the limit of the ice-box was reached earlier than expected and we were soon back on bully beef, salt horse and lime juice. The nutritional value of food was never a consideration, and not being a good eater, it didn't bother me much.

The 2nd Mate decided to have a shilling sweepstake on when the ship would reach the longitude of the Horn. The Old Man would deduct it from the account of wages at the end of the trip. The weather was fine and he kept the ship in as close as possible so Cape Horn could be seen from the bridge. I was at the wheel, darkness was setting in and the visibility wasn't all that good. TR came into the wheelhouse and said, 'Boy, you go out on the port wing and you'll see the Horn.' I strained my eyes and he came over and asked whether I could see it yet. 'I think I can, sir.' 'Of course you can,' T.R. replied, pointing into the distance. No sooner had I agreed than he disappeared into the chartroom, emerging again to announce that he had won the sweep himself. The 30 shillings proceeds were equally divided between the apprentices and added to our payoffs.

Although Montevideo looked a fine city, it gave the impression that Uruguay was a gun-toting lawless country. We stayed there ten days, discharging coal and preparing the holds for a grain cargo. Montevideo had risen to prominence early in the war with the scuttling of the German battleship Graf Spee and suicide of its commander, Captain Langsdorf, who shot himself.

On the first Sunday in port, TR received an invitation to attend a buffet at the British Consul's home with some of the other officers. He took the three apprentices along and told us to be properly dressed and wear clean shirts. We passed his inspection and promised not to drink too much. For the first time I really felt like a ship's officer. I was even more chuffed when TR said afterwards, 'For a change, you lot did well. God help you if you hadn't.' These were the nicest words he had said to us since the ship first sailed from Cardiff in August the previous year.

At that time everything in Montevideo was geared to the Uruguayan presidential election, due to take place at the beginning of December. Nobody seemed to be working apart from the girls in the local rags, who, I was told, were doing a great trade. Lorries, vans and cars, overloaded with highly-charged supporters of the various candidates, roared round the streets and avenues of the city, covering every square inch with enough leaflets for a countrywide British election. The streets were carpeted with paper, but as far as the girls were concerned they were paved with gold. Gunfire from supporters on the vehicles continued day and night. Everyone seemed to have a firearm and kept shooting into the air to generate the right atmosphere for a 1942 South American election.

The Consul said that there were more than 120 candidates for president. Each of them had to fight it on a major issue. One of them had promised that, if elected, nobody in Montevideo would have to walk uphill. The Consul felt that the worst thing that could happen to this particular candidate was to win, as anyone who did and didn't deliver his pre-election promises was for 'the chop', literally.

We left Montevideo on 4 December for the short passage up the River Plate to Rosario, and arrived there on the sixth. The mosquitoes were so bad that the ship had to anchor. The Argentine pilot couldn't stand out on the wing of the bridge. The Old Man, the mate and I at the wheel were completely covered with sheets, towels, and anything else available for protection against swarms of mossies which brought the ship to a standstill in the middle of the river. All the cabin portholes were closed as there wasn't a mosquito net anywhere on board. No other mosquito-infested place has ever seemed to compare with the night of 5 December 1942 in the Rio De La Plata. All I saw of Rosario were mosquitoes and grain, but those who managed to get ashore enjoyed wonderful hospitality from the large British community.

Roosevelt had put an embargo on the carriage of coal from the States to the Argentine, which suffered as a result. Our Montevideo cargo would have been very welcome in Rosario or Buenos Aires, where they had resorted to burning thousands of tons of grain to keep the power stations going.

Restrictive water depths in the river meant taking part cargo in Rosario, then down to Buenos Aires to top up. The ship arrived there on the tenth and sailed on 13 December. A couple of nights ashore convinced us the stories we had heard about the place were true. Most of the city was very nice, some of it wasn't, but it was all interesting. We covered the Boca, the Arches and other forbidding places seamen were expected to visit, but from which they may not all easily return. Three of us and one sparks seemed a formidable enough contingent. The 3rd Mate warned us to stay sober. Trigger-happy policeman, he claimed, scoured the streets late at night in their *collectivas*, ready to snatch drunken sailors and throw them into gaol. In the past, he continued, the Old Man had had to pay through the nose to bring them back to the ship. 'Believe me, I know,' he concluded. 'It happened to me when I was an apprentice.'

We had all heard of the infamous Canon Brady who liked young sailors, and ran the Mission in Buenos Aires. We wanted to see what he looked like and made this our first stop. After a large Argentine steak, we ended up under the Arches on the way back to the ship. In the place we visited, the downstairs was for dancing, upstairs for drinking and socialising. The socialising was different to anything we had seen before and it was interesting to watch.

A number of scantily dressed waitresses brought small glasses of beer up to the balcony from a downstairs bar. They were courteous and clearly very obliging, but we stuck to the beer. They seemed to be working on commission and on a shared basis with one another. When an agreement had been made to sit on a customer's lap another girl would arrive at ever shorter intervals with more beer for the distracted client. The cost depended on the time he took. We soon understood why the black and white chequered tablecloths were much too large for the size of the tables.

Near us, an old Argentinian was struggling away under the tablecloth. He was dressed in a tweed jacket with plus fours and a matching cap with a button on top, and looked like he was having a night off from his ranch in the Pampas. His face got redder and redder, the beers arrived more and more quickly, and his bill for drinks got bigger and bigger. He still hadn't made it when we left for the ship.

Buenos Aires was one of the most corrupt places ships visited. They had to conform to regulations not required elsewhere. The gangway had to be painted white with an oil lamp lashed onto the shore end. If the light blew out, the ship was fined. By a remarkable coincidence this happened frequently, even when there was no wind, and always as a policeman happened to be passing by. Rat guards were required on the shore end of all mooring ropes. It was amazing the number of times they fell off, also incurring a fine. There were many other 'offences' and the captain had to pay. The costs were expected and allowed for in his voyage disbursements.

The short stay in Buenos Aires ended on the 13 December and the ship sailed for Port of Spain, Trinidad. Since the Battle of the River Plate, Argie interest in the war at sea had subsided and events a couple of thousand miles away in the North Atlantic were of no concern. It mattered very much to a master of a ship about to sail the length of South America for the West Indies and passing through the most U-boat infested area of the Caribbean to get there. Steaming distance from Buenos Aires to Trinidad was about 4,500 miles and there was no updated submarine or raider information available. There was plenty activity above the Equator and parallel to the north coast of South America. This was more evident when we arrived at Trinidad, where many survivors from ships sunk in the Caribbean were waiting for berths back home. They signed on as supernumeraries and didn't care what ship it was as long as it eventually got to a UK port.

The three we took on board were DEMS gunners from different ships Two would supplement the guns' crew but the other wasn't fit for anything after an horrendous ordeal. He wouldn't sleep in the gunners' quarters or go anywhere down below when the ship was at sea. When his vessel was torpedoed, he was asleep in a hammock up on the boat deck and the blast in number three hold where it struck blew the covers off an adjacent bunker hatch. He was catapulted into the air, down the hold and washed out through the hole in the hull made by the torpedo. He was the only survivor.

We arrived Port of Spain, Trinidad on New Year's Day and by then had been at sea for almost nine months. The Hogmanay spirit wasn't as jolly as it had been in South Africa the previous year. Time ashore was limited and the ship moved from Port of Spain to the famous Pitch Lake in the south west of the island to load a consignment of asphalt before sailing on 12 January.

Date and Hour of the Occurrence	Place of the Occurrence, or situation by Latitude and Longitude at Sea.	Date of Entry.	Entries required by Act of Parliament.	Amount of Fine or Particulars inflicted.
29. 6. 42 9 A.M.	In Port. Basra	29.6.42	This is to certify that Chief Officer Donald Macdonald N° 2 reported fit for duty. J. G. Reid, Master. D. J. Macdonald, Mate.	
4. 4. 42 11 A.M.	In Port. Basra	4.4.42	This is to certify that Charles Runciman N° 8 Chief Engineer was this day discharged from hospital and now fit for his duties. J. G. Reid, Master. D. J. Macdonald, Mate.	
16. 4. 42 6 A.M.	Abadan	16.4.42	This is to certify that I have this day taken Apprentice George Gunn N° 24 to Hospital to be examined. After examination he reported he was suffering with dysentery and would have to remain in hospital. His clothes was packed, and taken with to hospital. His account of wages was paid up to todays date and balance deposited at H. B. M. Consulate. Balance of wages due £ Nil. Unemployment Card retained onboard for completion. J. G. Reid, Master. D. J. Macdonald, Mate.	
16. 4. 42 4 P.M.	In Port. Abadan	16.4.42	This is to certify that the following members of crew were taken to hospital for examination William Pearson N° 18 3rd Engineer and Kenneth Brown N° 4 3rd Officer also Leon Fessue Apprentice N° ... 3rd Engineer N° 10 had slight attack of fever but was able to travel with vessel and to be re-examined at next ...	

Date and Hour of the Occurrence	Place of the Occurrence, or situation by Latitude and Longitude at Sea.	Date of Entry.	Entries required by Act of Parliament.	Amount of Fine or Particulars inflicted.
18. 8. 42 10 A.M.	In Port. Calcutta	18.8.42	This is to certify that Donald John Macdonald 1st Mate N° 2 was again attended to by Shore Dr. As I did not like the look of the injured big toe I insisted on the 1st Mate being sent to hospital. Arrangements were duly made and said Seaman entered hospital to day at 6 P.M. J. G. Reid, Master. A. H. Livingstone, 2nd Mate.	✓
21. 8. 42 11 A.M.	In Port. Calcutta	21.8.42	This is to certify that George S. Gunn Apprentice N° 24 reported vessel, being discharged from hospital at Abadan, and now fit for normal duties. J. G. Reid, Master. A. H. Livingstone, 2nd Mate.	✓
22. 8. 42 9 A.M.	In Port. Calcutta	22.8.42	This is to certify that new Lascar crew joined vessel to day. All having been medically examined and vaccinated against Small Pox. Old crew discharged 16.8.42. J. G. Reid, Master. A. H. Livingstone, 2nd Mate.	
22. 8. 42 5 P.M.	In Port. Calcutta	22.8.42	This is to certify that Benjamin Broadhead Fireman N° 14 was examined by Naval Dr. who ordered his removal to hospital. Said Seaman having suspected Malaria. The Balance of his wages being paid to him, which amounted to £ R. 14. 6. His personal effects were taken to hospital with him. J. G. Reid, Master. A. H. Livingstone, 2nd Mate.	
22. 8. 42 8 P.M.	In Port. Calcutta	22.8.42	This is to certify that when I went up to hospital to get D. Donald John Macdonald 1st Mate N° 2 back to vessel I was informed he was unfit for duty as Surgeon had cut in on big toe of right foot. Further that they were operating on big toe on the 24.8.42.	

OFFICIAL LOG of the S.S. *Baron Renfrew*
from   towards

Date and Hour of the Occurrence.	Place of the Occurrence, or situation by Latitude and Longitude at Sea.	Date of Entry.	Entries required by Act of Parliament.
18.1.43 11 A.M.	In Port. GUANTANAMO Cuba	18.1.43	This is to certify that Fredrick Davis Deck Hand No 16 was examined by United States Navy Dr. He confirmed that the swelling which appeared when truss was removed was a rupture. After replacing gut, and truss, he recommended an operation when vessel reached U.K. Thos. F. Reid Master D J Macdonald mate
18.1.43 11 A.M.	In Port. GUANTANAMO Cuba	18.1.43	This is to certify that Apprentice George Gunn No 24 had five teeth extracted by United States Naval Dentist. The said Apprentice is to be examined tomorrow again for further teeth to be extracted Thos F. Reid Master D J Macdonald mate
19.1.43 10 A.M.	In Port. GUANTANAMO Cuba	19.1.43	This is to certify that Apprentice George Gunn No 24 had one tooth extracted Thos. F. Reid Master D J Macdonald mate

OFFICIAL LOG of the S.S. *Baron Renfrew*
from   towards

Date and Hour of the Occurrence.	Place of the Occurrence, or situation by Latitude and Longitude at Sea.	Date of Entry.	Entries required by Act of Parliament.	Amount of Wages or Forfeiture in each
20.1.43 10 A.M.	In Port. GUANTANAMO Cuba	20.1.43	This is to certify that Apprentice George Gunn No 24 was again examined by ships Dr & Dentist owing to his gums still bleeding. Same was attended to, and prescribed for, and bleeding has been stopped. Thos F. Reid Master D J Macdonald mate	
26.2.43 9-30 A.M.	In Port. Leith	26.2.43	This is to certify that Fredrick Davis No 16 Deck Hand and Stanley Gibson No 24 Deck Hand was this day signed off Articles D J Macdonald Mate Thos. F. Reid Master	
27.2.43 4 P.M.	In Port. Leith	27.2.43	This is to certify that Charles L. Roover No 19 Deck Hand, Charles Kane No 25 Deck Hand, and Albert Taylor No 26 Deck Hand were taken ashore by Military Authorities. I was unable to sign them off Articles as Shipping Office was closed.	

N.B.—Every entry in this Log-Book required by the Act must be signed by the Master and by the Mate or some other of the Crew and every entry of illness, injury or death must also be signed by the Surgeon or Medical Practitioner on board (if any); and every entry of wages due to, or of the sale of the effects of, any Seaman or Apprentice who has died must be signed by the Master and by the Mate and some other member of the Crew; and every entry of wages due to any Seaman who enters His Majesty's Service must be signed by the Master and by the Seaman or by the Officer authorised to receive the Seaman into such Service.

NOTE.—Reading over Entries of Offences.—The Master's especial attention is called to Section 228.(b) (c) and (d) of the Merchant Shipping Act, 1894, which is printed on page 2 of the blue cover on this Official Log-Book.

I certify that I have carefully examined this Official Log and find that no entries have been made on the pages subsequently to this certificate.

N.B.—Every entry in this Log-Book required by the Act must be signed by the Master and by the Mate or some other of the Crew and every entry of illness, injury or death must also be signed by the Surgeon or Medical Practitioner on board (if any); and every entry of wages due to, or of the sale of the effects of, any Seaman or Apprentice who has died must be signed by the Master and by the Mate and some other member of the Crew; and every entry of wages due to any Seaman who enters His Majesty's Service must be signed by the Master and by the Seaman or by the Officer authorised to receive the Seaman into such Service.   Thos F. Reid Master   D J Macdonald mate

NOTE.—Reading over Entries of Offences.—The Master's especial attention is called to Section 228.(b) (c) and (d) of the Merchant Shipping Act, 1894, which is printed on page 2 of the blue cover on this Official Log-Book.

MERCANTILE MARINE OFFICE 6 - MAR 1943 SOUTH SHIELDS

We left Trinidad fully loaded and arrived Guantanamo, Cuba on 17 January. Admiral King and his navy had started merchant ship convoys between American east coast ports and the West Indies. Guantanamo Bay was an ideal convoy assembly area and good shore facilities, such as medical help and assistance, were readily available by courtesy of the US Navy. Fred the gunlayer fell in Trinidad and ruptured himself and I had severe toothache. TR took us both ashore for attention. Fred was advised to have an operation as soon as the ship got to the UK. The naval dentist pulled out five of my teeth. By the time he had finished, I knew all about his liking for Glasgow, Sauchiehall Street, the Beresford Hotel where he was based before coming to Cuba, and the lovely Scottish broads he met there. Clearly, it wasn't just teeth he could pull.

I had to go back for another extraction and spent the next ten days trying to stop the flow of blood from my mouth. Most of the way up to New York I did my two-hour stints at the wheel beside an empty seven-pound jam tin and a wad of cotton wool. I had been called a bleeder before, but for different reasons.

We left Guantanamo on 24 January and sailed for New York in our first American convoy. There were more naval escorts than cargo vessels, and US Air Force cover for the whole 1,000 miles ensured a trouble free passage. The ship arrived off the Hudson River and anchored, awaiting daylight to dock. The halyards were frozen to the cleats and required thawing before the pilot flag could be hoisted. It was the first really cold weather I had experienced since going to sea in 1941. I remembered, then, Scott's words when he reached the South Pole: 'What a hellish place this is.' I soon discovered, in New York City in winter, that it was only the weather that was cold.

Aerial view of an Atlantic convoy. Photo taken in 1941 from a Fleet Air Arm escort plane.

(Imperial War Museum)

Leo and I made it ashore that evening after a 'tarpaulin muster' raised 50 cents. It was more than enough for two return fares anywhere on the New York Underground. We received a nice welcome form the ladies at the Seaman's Mission near Battery Park. They kindly gave us a woollen sweater and a diddy bag for each of four apprentices. Diddybags contained an assortment of tooth brushes, toothpaste, razors, shaving soap, socks and gloves. They were left over from Christmas and New Year, and with a North Atlantic winter ahead, they were very much appreciated.

There was only one more night ashore before sailing from New York in convoy for the UK. We saw a lot of Manhattan in a short time and hoped it wouldn't be long before we saw a lot more. New York was the most fascinating place we had been to anywhere in the world and it looked likely to be able to live up its reputation as 'the biggest, the best and the worst', and we intended sometime to prove it for ourselves.

The convoy across the Western Ocean from New York to Loch Ewe took 18 days and arrived there on 21 February for dispersal. A coastal convoy from there through the Pentland Firth and down to Leith took three days and the ship anchored off there after almost a year at sea. It was a long voyage; we had 'tramped' a complete circumnavigation of the world and were glad to be home at last. My pent-up feelings took over when Sparks handed me his earphones and said, 'Listen to this.' It was Vera Lynn singing 'We'll Meet Again'. I cried.

After discharging the grain in Leith, the ship went to dry dock on the Tyne. I was allowed home from Leith for two nights. I missed the last train from Edinburgh to Glasgow and, not wanting to take a chance by going back aboard the ship, stayed in a Prince's Street hotel near the railway station. The next morning, inevitably I overslept.

Most of the gunners were taken off the ship and we were sorry to lose Fred from Battersea. We had seen a lot of the world in the previous 18 months and he was a good shipmate ashore and afloat. After one farewell night in Leith, I was left to my own devices when I was ashore.

Between day work on board the ship, the depleted wartime rail services and no more travel warrants until the voyage ended at the Tyne, there was no alternative to a night out in Edinburgh. I only knew it as the capital of Scotland, and compared to Glasgow it was considered a serious, sombre and rather boring place. Everything stopped or closed by 9 o'clock and I found myself well, after that time, in a small intimate club on Prince's Street. Considering the war and rationing problems, the customers were well up to what one would expect in Edinburgh; particularly the young lady with whom I had a drink. Unfortunately, there was also a time limit there and we had to leave.

The long cold walk from Edinburgh to the docks at Leith in the blackout was a much less inviting prospect than to be put up for the night until the first trams in the morning. It was an offer I just could not resist.

The apartment, just off Prince's Street, was comfortable enough to be called luxurious, and the lady who occupied it was very hospitable. I was about to fall asleep when I was told the upkeep of the apartment and school boarding fees cost money. I gave her my last ten shillings and kept sixpence tram fare back to the ship. She didn't seem overwhelmingly grateful, but I thought it was better value than the bed and breakfast I recently had at the County Hotel around the corner.

She was sound asleep when I left at five, The last words I heard her say was something about being more careful in the future. She obviously hadn't learned to differentiate between a well-dressed, tanned young sailor and a hard-up ship's apprentice.

We arrived at the Tyne on 5 March and articles were closed that day at Mill Dam shipping office in South Shields. Captain T.R. Reid signed himself off and went home for a well-earned rest. The strict disiplinary measures he enforced on board the ship at all times applied to every member of the crew, from the chief officer down to the lowest rating. Everyone had to do his job in strict accordance with the signed agreement. All the time he was there the *Renfrew* was run as efficiently as any tramp steamer could be; all hands knew exactly where they stood. His immediate successor had a hard act to follow, and never quite succeeded. The difference between an experienced Lascar crew master and one only used to white crew ships was readily apparent. TR wanted a break and a change, but we didn't want him to go.

The vessel dry-docked at the Brigham and Cowan shipyard in South Shields for survey and general overhaul. The new mate sent me home for a week's leave, and when I got back to the Tyne the ship was still in dry dock. Immediately I arrived home in Glasgow, my mother insisted I had a decent haircut. It was the first time I had seen a female barber in a gents' hairdressers and I said that I didn't like it. I was reminded that it was women who kept the home fires burning and worked the munition and aircraft factories when men were away at war. My mother considered that women made better barbers than did Chinese carpenters on tramp steamers.

When I got back to South Shields it wasn't surprising to find women assisting joiners and plumbers and doing other labouring jobs around the ship and dry dock. In our long time at sea, lots of things had changed ashore in the UK.

That was the first of many trips to South Shields and the other Tyne ports, and it was always good news to hear that the ship was to load or discharge at one of them. I got on with Geordies, and Newcastle was the nearest English port to Glasgow.

Two years of war at sea could take its toll. The condition of the *Baron Elgin*, photographed at Funchal, Madeira, in 1942, is typical. The ship is seen here disembarking survivors from Convoy SL 125. *(Photograph courtesy of Craig Carter)*

Convoy SL 125 – West Africa to UK: 37 ships, 12 sunk. During the U-boat attack the *Elgin* turned round to stop and rescue survivors from other vessels which had been sunk or abandoned. A surfaced U-boat, seeing what was happening, withheld its fire and circled the ship allowing the *Elgin* to complete the rescue operation and take the survivors to Madeira. Early on in the war there were a number of similar acts of mercy, but on Hitler's orders and after the entry of Japan into the conflict, these were few and far between.

CHAPTER 7   New York! New York!

The ship was at the Tyne for more than a month. A relief master opened new articles on 9 March and TR's successor joined just before we sailed on 8 April. It was back round to Oban via Methil for another deep-sea convoy across the Western Ocean to Halifax, then down the coast to New York. We berthed at Brooklyn and were chartered by Bull Lines of New York to take a general cargo to the West Indies. General cargoes took a long time to load and the ship stayed in Brooklyn for about two weeks. It was a great chance to get to know New York City, and with most evenings free, we made the best of it.

My first duty was to visit my mother's cousin, who lived with an Italian family near Madison Square Gardens. He wasn't in and I was told that he wouldn't be back that night. I opted for Times Square and Broadway. There were uniforms everywhere, as Uncle Sam had ensured that most entertainment on the Great White Way was available free for soldiers, sailors and airmen, and as much Coco Cola as they wanted to drink. All we needed for a night on the town in Manhattan was the ten-cent tube fare from Brooklyn. There was no free beer on tap, but at a nickel a glass in any bar on Broadway it was affordable.

We soon got to know where to go and not to go in New York. The only real no-go part of the city in 1943 was Harlem. New York was probably the easiest and least costly city in the world to get around. We visited and enjoyed places we knew about but had only seen in films. Cinemas on Broadway included live stage shows in their nightly programmes and, having had the opportunity to see Jimmy Dorsey and Gene Krupa and their bands in the flesh, we understood why they were so famous. Gene Krupa was at the time defending himself against allegations of drug-taking to enhance his performance, which from what we saw at the Roxy, didn't seem necessary. A midnight movie took about two hours, which allowed another couple of hours in Jack Dempsey's Broadway bar just down the street, before it closed for cleaning at 4.00am.

Five minutes after the bell was rung for the end of the round in Dempsey's, everyone was out in the street. I never saw anyone refuse a bouncer's invitation to leave the premises. They all looked like recruits from Jack's stable of former heavyweight sparring partners. He sat at a table, signing photos at a dollar a time. There was no shortage of customers, but by the time I got back to New York with a dollar to spare Jack had retired. During the war, Dempsey's was a popular meeting place for British merchant seamen and there was no likelihood of any trouble inside or outside the bar.

Mother's cousin worked in the Bankers Club of America at the lower end of Broadway. I saw a member ask a waitress to fetch cigarettes. She walked all of five yards to the kiosk and brought over a ten-cent pack of Lucky Strike. He gave her a $10 bill and told her to keep the change. In New York, it wasn't only skyscrapers that were big.

I attended a dance organised by the ladies of New York for officers and crews of visiting ships. They not only supplied partners but insisted on one to one introductions. Mine was from Brooklyn, and her claim to fame was that she knew Dutch Schultz. I had never heard of him, but I soon learned that he was the New York City crime boss who was shot dead sitting at a bar, minding his own business. I saw her home on the tube to Brooklyn and was surprised to find, she lived on a tree-lined avenue. We arranged to meet the following evening at Times Square. When I got there, I realised that it was clearly no place to try to meet anyone, and I never saw the Brooklyn girl again.

It was said that one in every ten men who passed you in Times Square had been up the river in Sing Sing. I stood there watching and counting, but there were too many candidates to be able to select just one from any ten.

I then met 'Lieutenant' Hodder, working with his girl friend around the clubs and bars on Broadway. She photographed the customers and he took the money and had the prints quickly developed and delivered back to the pub or club. They invited me to go round with them. It was another interesting New York evening. Hodder wore a Merchant Navy officer's cap badge and not a Royal Navy one. There being no lieutenants on merchant ships, his story reeked of bull. All the con men I

'Lieutenant' Hodder (right) with George Gunn, at Jim O'Neill's Magpie Cafe in New York, May 1942.

met at sea were nice guys and Hodder was no exception. I had an enjoyable night in their company and learned a lot about the twilight world of New York City, as the photograph of us taken by his girl friend in Jim O'Neill's Magpie Café clearly shows.

I deduced that my companion for the evening was a steward on some British merchant vessel, who had jumped ship either in San Francisco or Los Angeles and thought it easier to lose himself in New York than on the west coast of the United States. I wished him well and got back aboard the ship at Brooklyn, in time to start work but with little enthusiasm.

It is unbelievable to those who have visited New York in recent years to be told that, in the early 1940s, a person could walk all the way down Atlantic Avenue in Brooklyn at three in the morning with no fear of being mugged or accosted. New York then was as safe as any city or

town in the UK. The violence shown on American films was usually between gangs who fought among themselves. It was felt that the FBI and New York Police Department let them get on with it as long as it didn't affect the general public, and the more damage they did to one another's organisations, the better.

Before we sailed on 22 May in another American convoy bound for Guantanamo, there was enough time ashore to get to know Manhattan. We went everywhere and tried everything, but always ended on Broadway, usually at Dempsey's. Before midnight his beer cost 10 cents, between then and 2 a.m. it was 12, and after that until they closed at 4 o'clock it went up to 15. An early breakfast of spaghetti and meatballs on the way back aboard blunted any need for a plate of ship's porridge before turning to.

The dances we had so far attended in New York were well-organised, formal and uninteresting. Encouraged by a billboard outside a hall advertising Mugsie Spannier and his band, Leo and I bought a few ten-cent tickets and had a go at taxi dancing. This involved more close physical contact than dancing, and when the tickets finished so did our partners. Their promise of things to come if we bought another dollar's worth each was sufficient inducement to leave.

The convoy arrived at Guantanamo on 28 May and the ship carried on independently to Ciudad Trujillo in Haiti and moored alongside on 1 June. We worked cargo for eight days and went on to Barahona to load sugar for home.

Ships tied up literally alongside in Ciudad Trujillo. The mooring ropes were made fast to bollards on the main street and cargo was discharged or loaded right there. We were advised not to go wandering around ashore on our own at night. That restricted the evening entertainment to a couple of bodegas across the road. They offered music, girls and rum. It was also more comfortable to go there in a group. The Renfrew was the only foreign vessel in port at the time and, having an Indian crew, the number of potential customers for the bodegas' evening entertainment was limited. We could see from the ship that they were also open for business throughout the day.

The sugar was loaded from lighters, with the ship anchored well off Barahona. We were there for eight days and never saw the place. It was hot and sticky, and each apprentice was responsible for dunnageing one of the holds before cargo was stowed. The huge coloured dockers individually lifted 200-lb. bags of sugar from a platform in the centre of the hold and carried them out into the wings. We had to ensure that none of the bags came into direct contact with the steel surfaces of the ship. We used lengths of dunnage wood and large reed mats and wrapped them around stanchions and against the vessel's shell plating. To keep up with the stowage, we worked the same 12-hour shifts down the holds as the dockers, and were relieved for a meal and a 'smokoe' by the 3rd mate. One week down the hold with the Barahona cargo-wallahs put me off eating brown sugar for a long time after.

There was an abundance of fruit ashore in Barahona, but the ship was too far off for us to get any. The chandler delivered some grapefruit for ship's stores. I went along to the pantry and asked the steward for one for the apprentices. The Old Man shouted from the dining saloon, 'What does that boy want? Send him in here.' I was told that I would only get a grapefruit when I had a ticket.

Photo taken from HMS *Eglinton* in 1941 of Outward Bound convoy assembling

(National Maritime Museum, London)

We spent three days in Guantanamo, waiting for convoy. Every time I saw the place, I thought of the teeth that were needlessly extracted on our first call, and wondered how many others had similarly suffered at the hands of the resident US navy dentist.

The convoy from Cuba to New York took one week, and we arrived on 30 June. The ship was only in port for a couple of days and, for the first time abroad, there was some crew's mail from home. The 3rd Mate's letter contained bad news. His engagement to a Paisley undertaker's daughter was off. I wasn't surprised, but he was distraught.

Before sailing, he had confessed to her all the bad things he had done since going to sea. This included an eight-day stay in Huelva, Spain, where he and Sparks met two señoritas and bet each other on how often they could make love to them in that time. Sparks managed twelve, but the 3rd Mate won with fourteen. The undertaker's daughter wasn't complimentary about his prowess, but assured him of her forgiveness and that the wedding would go ahead as planned when the ship got back home.

We left New York on 2 July with enough sugar for a week's ration for everyone in the UK after all the by-products had been extracted. Someone said that in wartime there were more than fifty of these, some of which were used in munitions factories. I never pursued the subject, but as with other unlikely stories at the time, there was no reason to disbelieve it.

The ship sailed up the East River to Long Island Sound, then through the Cape Cod Canal to Boston. From there, it continued to Halifax for another convoy across the Western Ocean to Loch Ewe, in Scotland. We joined a coastal convoy down to Methil and on to London to discharge the cargo, arriving there on 29 July.

In coastal convoys, I was on the port Marlins and until then had never had the opportunity to fire a shot in anger. The chance came when the convoy was almost at the Thames estuary. We were last in the starboard column and heard the faint drone of an aircraft coming up astern. As soon as the shape was visible, the mate told me to fire. I did – and others followed – until the plane disappeared in the half light. The mate said it was definitely an enemy aircraft, as it was flying well inside the minimum height allowed over a convoy. The Old Man arrived back from convoy de-briefing and said 'I have a message from Coastal Command: "good shooting, you bastards. You hit my rear gunner".'

The London dockers took one look at the 200lb bags of sugar and refused to discharge them, saying they were too heavy to handle. They then walked off the ship. It seemed a most ungrateful attitude, considering the vessel had steamed 5,000 miles through submarine-infested waters to get it there, and that the lives of 60 men had been put at risk to do so.

The following morning, lorryloads of troops arrived alongside, under the command of a very senior army officer. He told the mate they had orders to get all the sugar off and three days in which to do it. The mate asked where the stupid order had come from and was told that it had come directly from Winston Churchill. 'You don't really think, old man,' the officer said, 'that he would allow 5,000 tons of essential food supplies to be left lying on a ship in the middle of London when half the population is starving, do you?'.

The sugar was all discharged inside three days. The holds were swept up and cleaned out ready for the next cargo, wherever it might come from. The mate was very pleased and complimented the officer on his men's achievement. 'That's alright,' the officer replied. 'These men can do anything, including winning a war.'

Having recently dry-docked on the Tyne and done a short 15-week trip to the West Indies, the ship was ready for a quick turn around and back to sea. There was always the possibility of another long voyage, so I asked for leave, was paid off in London, and joined my second ship in Greenock after two wonderful weeks at home in Glasgow. In a way, I was sorry to leave the Renfrew, but two years on one vessel during the war was a long time. I hoped the next ship would be as lucky.

Southbound convoy steaming off the Wold, 1941

The bombing which paralysed London had the opposite effect on Glasgow. Big-name bands, variety acts and theatre shows transferred to safer venues north of the border. Although Glasgow was never the capital of Scotland, throughout the war it was the entertainment capital of Britain. It was the ideal place for home leave.

I was still pleased to get back to sea and, after two weeks, I joined the *Yarborough* at Greenock. The only other vessel requiring an apprentice was owned by the ministry and operated by the Baron Line. She was going on convoy work between the UK and Russia. I asked for my service in the tropics to be considered, and I was sent to the old three-islander, built in 1928.

We sailed from Greenock on 20 August, arrived in Cardiff on the twenty-second, and loaded coal for the Mediterranean. What, with coal bunkering, the cargo, the rusty hull, decks, bulwarks and hatch coamings, the Yarborough looked in every way like a white-crewed tramp steamer which had sailed the North Atlantic since war started.

It took just four days to load and sail from Cardiff. We cleared the Bristol Channel on 27 August, then headed out into the Atlantic in company with other vessels from Milford to join a south-bound convoy for Gibraltar. The weather wasn't good, and with the restraining effect of ships like the Yarborough, the slow convoy was slower than expected. The ships dispersed at Gibraltar and we sailed independently to Bizerta, arriving there on 14 September. After dodging several vessels scuttled in the approach channel by the recently retreating German Army, we anchored in the lake at Bizerta, just over 50 miles from Tunis.

The pilot who took us in was like a cat on hot bricks, continually changing his orders and alternating between French and English, with the occasional phrase in German. The Old Man told me to ignore him. 'Stay in the middle and steer round the wrecks, or we'll end up joining them. Who knows, perhaps he's one of Hitler's secret weapons.'

British and American troops from Bizerta and Tunis had landed in Sicily. They were still embarking on landing craft for the 100-mile trip across, before heading on to Italy. We followed on 16 September and

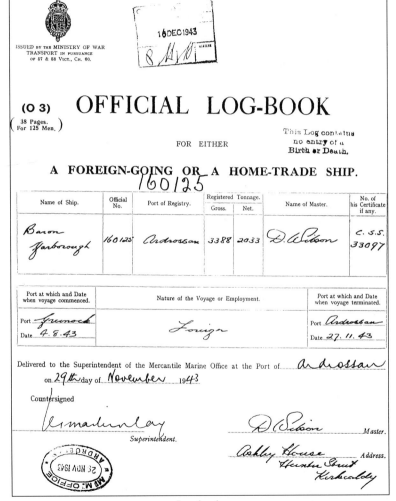

Log book.

arrived Palermo on the seventeenth, with the cargo of best Welsh coal. Apart from one inquisitive Luftwaffe plane, the passage was uneventful. He flew around, well out of range, and either didn't have anything left to drop or didn't think it worth the trouble.

The ship berthed at the unloading pier on 23 September and didn't finish discharging and leave Palermo until 11 October. It must have been a nice city, until they decided to flatten it before the troops arrived. An immense amount of high explosive was dropped there and one sizeable vessel was blown right out of the water onto the quay wall.

Many years after, I met a former Luftwaffe pilot, who said he fought in Sicily during the invasion. He mentioned the ship on the wall at Palermo, which was convincing enough; but his account of air raids on London wasn't. He said that he didn't like dropping bombs on innocent civilians and that he jettisoned them in the English Channel on the way back to France.

The cargo took two weeks to discharge. By then, British and Canadian forces had crossed the Straits of Messina between Sicily and Italy and bitter fighting was taking place further up the Italian coast at Salerno. These were the first successful allied landings on enemy occupied territory in mainland Europe and there we were, berthed in the middle of it, with a cargo of coal.

The weather was pleasantly warm and there was plenty of time to explore Palermo, but only during the day. The Yanks had imposed a 9 o'clock curfew and after that only their military police were allowed on the streets. The 22,000 troops occupying the city looked too fresh and well-dressed to have fought their way through north Africa before getting to Sicily. In order to remain alive, we stayed on board after dark. Merchant Navy uniforms weren't worn ashore in neutral or occupied countries, and the risk of being mistaken for an erring Sicilian by some trigger-happy MP wasn't worth taking.

Landing craft packed with troops regularly called at Palermo on their way to Salerno and other points on the Italian coast. In the evenings we sat on the quay wall, watching and wondering what lay ahead of them when they arrived.

Bombed-out shopkeepers erected makeshift stalls in the streets. They had little to sell except sweetmeats and Marsalla wine. There seemed to be plenty of that around and at 100 lire a bottle, four could be bought for £1. The downside was that crew members got a taste for it and could afford more than was good for them. Throughout the ship's stay in port, the two apprentices worked over the side with the deck crowd, trying to get rid of the thick rust which covered the entire shell plating. Although there were no serious accidents on the stages, the previous night's Marsalla consumption led to a steady loss of chipping hammers and red lead brushes down into the harbour.

By then, Sicily was fully occupied by invading forces. Intermingling with local residents, promenading the streets and boulevards of Palermo and haggling with vendors was one of the few pastimes available to American troops. They acted more like tourists than members of a conquering army, and the Sicilians took full advantage by charging a small fortune for a limited range of cheap-looking souvenirs. The Germans, when they were there, just took what they wanted from their Italian 'allies'.

It was a nice change to meet four members of the Black Watch in Palermo. Their regiment was engaged across the Straits of Messina in Italy and they were batmen for high-ranking officers, visiting the city for talks with 'blood-and-guts Patton' and some of his commanders. The soldiers were told to find accommodation, make themselves comfortable, and report back to US Army headquarters in a week. They set up home in one of the best hotels in Palermo, part of which was still standing.

Two of them were from Dundee and two from Edinburgh. They started at Alamein, with the 51st Highland Division fought right across North Affrica to Tunis then Sicily and were now about to make their way up through Italy. Curly said it would take some time but it looked the only way they would get back home.

Tanned by the African sun and with their uniform caps sporting the regiment's distinguishing Red Hackles, they stood out from all the other military personnel in Palermo. They couldn't get into any American Army club in the city and hadn't had a cup of tea or a decent meal for days. We took them on board the ship and rectified that. As it was Saturday, the cook and the rest of the crew were either ashore or asleep, and a large 'black pan' full of all-in stew was simmering on the galley

Baron Yarborough, which survived the war. (1928-1965).
(Photograph of vessel in new condition – arriving UK with a cargo of pitprops.)
Built by Ayrshire Dockyard, Irvine in 1928. Sold to Italy in 1963 and scrapped there in 1965.

stove. It consisted of bits and pieces left from previous meals and was there to satisfy firemen coming up from the stokehold. This time it satisfied the Black Watch.

Before sailing from Palermo we were invited to a farewell party at the hotel. This consisted of lots of chocolate and marzipan cakes and bottles of Marsalla decoratively arrayed around the room. We sang without music, reminisced about home, and arranged to meet in Scotland after the War. Like most of these dates, it never happened. While we were singing, the door opened and a slightly inebriated Yank walked in saying, 'Oh! good! A party!' Curly excused himself, propelled him out of the room and threw him down the stairs. He never came back. Without money, how did they manage to get so much to eat and drink? As one of them explained, 'Like other places we've been through, this is an occupied country. And anyway, these people are making enough out of the Yanks to pay for ours as well.'

We left the hotel two hours after curfew time. Luckily we knew the side streets to use to get back to the ship. The wallet containing my seaman's identity card was taken from my back pocket in Palermo. It would have been very inconvenient to be picked up by MPs the night before sailing and be baled out by the Old Man in the morning. The good conduct bonus couldn't survive that.

The ship sailed on 11 October and arrived back to anchor in the lake at Bizerta the next day. The steward was running out of food. There was none in Palermo or Bizerta, so we had gone from the frying pan into the fire. The military authorities ashore had more to think about than storing a tramp ship in need. When a ship's crew were hungry, they didn't appreciate that and the captain and steward were always to blame. I was told to go to Bizerta in one of the lifeboats with a couple of sailors and lots of cigarettes and tobacco on a changey-changey mission for food. An army quartermaster gave us three bags of potatoes and 'enough pumpkins to see us back to Blighty'.

After ten days in Bizerta we port-hopped to Gibraltar, with short spells at anchor in Bone, Phillipsville, Bougie and Algiers. Sweeping the ship from stem to stern with a wire stretched underneath the hull, was a daily exercise on British ships lying at anchor in Gibraltar Harbour. Algeciras, just across the Bay in Spain, was a base for German and Italian frogmen, who attached limpet mines to the undersides of vessels. We left Gibraltar after five days and docked at the nearby Spanish port of Huelva to load copper ore for the UK.

An ore cargo is poured into the holds and a ship is down to its marks in no time. It took three days to load and we sailed from Huelva on 12 November. It had been my first time ashore in Spain. There were no doubts among my shipmates about the country's lack of neutrality, and we were advised to be careful during our time there.

We found the Spanish people very pleasant and helpful. Robert and I felt quite comfortable in Huelva and enjoyed out first night ashore. The following evening, we returned to the same bodega and were immediately joined for a drink by the same three señoritas. Four rough-looking characters came into the tavern and two of the girls went right over to talk to them. The other one said, 'Franco's men, very bad, we look after them, you go quick.' We went. We discovered later that they were members of a Spanish Brigade, fighting for the Germans on the Russian Front. Their leave in Huelva was spent looking for British seamen and beating them up. We didn't go ashore there again.

We joined a homeward-bound convoy shortly after leaving Gibraltar on 13 November and the attack by U-boats and German aircraft started well out in the Atlantic. Some ships were torpedoed, others bombed and strafed, and the first radio message received on the bridge was that one of the naval escort vessels had been torpedoed and that they were trying to tow her to the Azores.

An account of the action is given by Ernie North in Kenneth Poolman's book *The British Sailor*. He was appointed to the sloop *Chanticleer*, no. UO5, which was building at William Denny's in Dumbarton. This was a vast change from sailing on HMS *Revenge* and HMS *Hood*, two of his previous vessels.

His first comments about the new ship were: a neat little sloop, not exactly a fleet greyhound but well armed and capable of handing out a terrific wallop down aft in the sub-hunting season. I liked her from the start. The officers were a great lot and my particular messmates a grand bunch. The Seamen POs knew their job and soon trained up their branch, 40 per cent of whom had never been to sea before.

After about twenty months in commission we took a convoy from

Newfoundland to the UK from which we were detattched to join another coming up from Gibraltar. It was mid-November and we all thought that a bit of sun would be just the job, and what nice people they were back in the Liver Buildings!

We joined the other convoy in the forenoon watch somewhere near the Azores. It was a glorious morning but we were told German aircraft and subs were around. About 1220 I went down to the Mess, had my tot and dinner, when there was a sound of depth charges in the distance. The ship altered course and increased speed and the submarine alarm went almost at once.

A convoy escort's nightmare – excessive smoke from the steamers, making visual detection easier.

(*National Maritime Museum, London*)

As we done hundreds of times before, everyone rushed to their action stations; hatches were closed, fans and ventilators were shut, and within one minute *Chanticleer* was ready to defend the convoy.

My action station was officer of the quarters on the two foremost twin 4in mountings. The guns crews told me a sub had been sighted astern of the convoy by those already closed up. I made a quick check round the mountings to make sure they had the right ammo, range and deflection dials at zero, and everything ready to open fire. We could hear the HSD searching for thr U-boat and the voice of the skipper ordering the sectors to be swept by the Asdics.

Orders came a bit quicker now. 'Follow Director. Load, load, load.' All guns were loaded and the gunlayers and trainers followed their dial pointers. We started our run on the submerged U-boat and could plainly hear the echoes right down to the HSDs.

'Instantaneous echo!' A shallow pattern had been ordered and the gunner normally on X gun had already moved down the quarterdeck to take charge of the depth charge party. As I neared X gun, the first charges were exploding astern.

At this point, with a tremendous roar, the whole quarterdeck seemed to disintergrate upwards in a jumbled mass and a wave of pressure and heat hit me. The ship shuddered horribly and rolled to port, then slowly came upright, moving unnaturally. We had been well and truly torpedoed. I thought, a helluva lot of people have just died.

The young depth-charge telephone number was sitting on the deck by the starboard screen, his phones still on his hand and looking in a bad way – the only man left alive on the quarterdeck. The ship's rudder, which weighed between 30 and 50 tons, had flown up into the air and come down like a great butcher's cleaver, thudding into the upper deck, a few feet from the lad on the phones. Both after oerlikon power mountings and all the upper deck had gone, and the cabins and offices below were open to the sea and sky. The prop shafts were sticking out of the wreckage and loose deck charges hung around in all directions.

I returned to the guns up for'ard. The upper deck was littered with debris from aft and there were huge ridges and dents around the funnel. In various places there were also the horrible remains of our late messmates. A young officer was found alive, just, in the wreckage of the cabin flat aft, and we were lucky the weather was fine. All the boats were holed, and some of the carley rafts damaged, but the damage control party amidships and the engine room staff were shoring up the bulkhead between the engine room and the boiler room. At the guns we remained closed-up. The remains of one of the oerlikons was on the forecastle and we ditched that and a lot of other wreckage over the side.

Soon after I returned to the mounting we picked up another U-boat, bearing on our starboard side. A Sunderland then flew overhead, circled the ship and asked if they could take pictures. They were brusquely told to go and look for the U-boats that were going to slap another fish into us.

One of our chummy ships in the group, HMS Crane, then came up to assist us and we prpared to abandon ship; Crane being asked to sink us by gunfire. The men were advised not to go below decks as she might decide to leave us at ant moment, but someone decided we needed some fags, and a carton of Chyrchman's No. 1 appeared on the upper deck from the canteen. Our canteen manager, also a dear shipmate, was dead, and if the ship was to be sunk, who was there to complain?

While the Crane was waiting for us, another torpedo was fired and she attacked an echo at least once. She was obviously in danger and moved off again. The skipper told us a tug was on its way to see if it could help. In a frenzy of activity, we began lightening the ship. Everything that was ditchable was ditched. Everything that was unscrewable was unscrewed and thrown overboard.

I, God knows why, decided to cut down a stubby little mast with a saw. We had only about three or four bodies available to bury, and a short service was held and we committed our dear shipmates to the deep. There were over thirty killed in all, and on a small ship with a very close knit set of officers and men, it was a crushing blow. Not all small ships reached the happy state of understanding we had.

*   *   *

The *Yarborough* was in a vulnerable condition, loaded down to its marks with a heavy cargo of ore and 50 depth charges secured on the after well deck along the sides of the hatches. They were put on board to

Baron Yarborough, and hungry gulls.

help replenish convoy escort vessels and until then hadn't been required. We thought this was just another illogical job to which merchant ships were often subjected during a war. For a corvette or destroyer to come alongside a cargo ship sailing in the middle of a convoy and transfer depth charges from one to the other under most weather conditions, seemed impractical. Both vessels would have to maintain courses and speeds and the seamen on one of them had no experience of an operation such as that. Until then, there were no concerns at having the depth charges on board. In the early 1940s, without a fatalistic attitude to life, it was better to stay ashore than go to sea. Paddy, our Irish bosun from Arklow, had his fair share. He was an old sailing-ship man but wasn't at sea all the time. In 1920, he joined the Black and Tans and was paid a pound a day by the British Government to shoot his own countrymen. He claimed that it was the best job he had ever had. When the dive bombers started their 'work' on the convoy, I asked him about the depth charges. He told me not to worry about them. 'If one goes off, lad,' he said, 'you won't know anything about it.'

That U-boats could torpedo a fast anti-submarine vessel so easily and early didn't bode well for the slow merchant ships in the convoy.

By the middle of November 1943 enemy attacks on convoys had decreased considerably, and in that month only 15 ships, totalling 62,000 tons, were lost. One year before, in November 1942, 76 ships, totalling 475,000 tons were sunk. Although Germany was losing the battle of the Atlantic, it was still harassing convoys.

In the next column on our port beam was the Blue Star/Lamport & Holt cargo liner, *Delius*. The ship immediately astern of her looked like a McLay, McIntyre tramp steamer, which was hit as they were lowering lifeboats. The vessel had broached to and was being dive-bombed and strafed with gunfire from attacking planes. I shouted to the mate when a periscope broke the water between us and Delius, before disappearing again. The mate said the U-boat was probably as surprised as we were to see where he was.

The action went on all day and looked like continuing throughout the night. *Delius* was hit and dropped back out of the convoy. I had watched what looked like a small plane flying low over the ships in that column. and shouted again to the mate, 'Look, sir! A Spitfire!' 'You daft bugger.

That's not a Spitfire. It's a bomb. Fire at it.' I kept firing until it was almost abeam. It hovered right above the *Delius*'s bridge, then fell with a huge explosion and everything disappeared in a cloud of smoke. I could see the derricks in front of the bridge curling up and the ship started to drop back. Another flying bomb fell just short of our stern, lifting it out of the water. It looked like we were going down bow first without taking a direct hit, but the old ship recovered and came back on an even keel. Planes carrying radio controlled bombs flew well out of range of ships' AA armament. Although we could see them above the thin cloud cover, nothing could be done; it was a matter of waiting and hoping. The fleeting clouds must have caused the bomb-aimer to drop ours a few seconds too soon.

Until then, glider bombs were unknown to anyone on the ship. The first ones were used about a month earlier on Convoy UGS18, bound from the States to Gibraltar. They were dropped by Dornier 217 aircraft, although the planes attacking us looked like Heinkels. There was too much happening to identify anything accurately. We learned much later that German glider bombs could reach speeds up 400 miles an hour and carried 1,100 lbs of high explosive. The quota of one per plane per ship favoured us that time.

On the perimeter of the convoy, action between escorts and subs continued throughout the night, but when daylight came there was no sign of any other ships. What was left of the convoy had disappeared. Like us they would be on their own, unescorted and steaming at 8 or 9 knots towards the UK. We were bound for Ardrossan, in Scotland, the ship's port of registry, to discharge the cargo. It seemed a long way off.

The 48-hour ordeal in convoy had its effect on crew members. The abysmal conditions under which sailors and firemen lived on this ship were sources of complaint throughout the trip. Those on board were crammed together under the forecastle head with no comfort or privacy, and the food they lived on was the worst I saw on any ship in my career. For a period of time, meals were limited to corned beef, pumpkin, and potatoes. The 66-year-old cook's long experience at sea on tough old tramps saved the day on many occasions. We had fried corned beef for breakfast, made into a pie for dinner, and 'neat' with chips at teatime. Everyone on board just wanted home and off the ship.

The master seldom came up on the bridge during and after the attacks. He just walked from one side of the lower bridge to the other, wearing a lifejacket.

The 1st Mate had been bumped off a couple of times before and remained up on the bridge. In between his watches, he lay on the chartroom settee. He was a very decent man and I felt sorry for him when he asked whether there was anything to drink in our cabin. I gave him a bottle of cherry brandy, bought in Huelva to take home. At the time, he needed it more than anyone else. I secretly hoped the Old Man had previously been bumped off as well, as it would account for his unusual behaviour.

The ship plodded on for several anxious days and we were very relieved to get into Ardrossan on 27 November. It was a bad trip all round. The mate told me to go home for three days, until the cargo was discharged. It looked like another quick turnround and back again to the Med, or across the Western Ocean to the States. At the time, neither prospect seemed very inviting on this particular ship.

When I arrived home in Glasgow, my mother said I wasn't looking quite as well as after the last trip. She had saved up her ration coupons and bought some corned beef as a homecoming treat, then told me to go and see the doctor. He didn't think I looked very good either and asked about the trip. I told him. He suggested nervous dyspepsia. He wrote a note to the 'Ship and Owners', recommending two weeks at home.

My younger brother volunteered to go down to the vessel with the doctor's note. I gave him train fare to Ardrossan and a sketch of the cabin showing where my gear was stowed. He told the mate I was sick and wouldn't be coming back. 'I don't blame him'; came the reply.

A couple of weeks doing the rounds of Glasgow dance halls, cinemas and shows was a great pick-me-up, and I joined the Forbes in Glasgow in the middle of December 1943.

CHAPTER 9   The *Baron Forbes*: Scotch whisky to Lisbon and beyond

The *Forbes* was the best known foreign-going vessel trading to the Clyde. Built in 1915, she was the oldest ship in the company: a German prize which was surrendered to Britain at the end of the First War and ran regularly between Glasgow, Lisbon and Huelva from 1922. For the previous ten years she had been under the command of the legendary Captain Lachie McPhail. Mr Arthur the chief engineer, had also been on the ship for ten years and his 2nd engineer was the longest-serving member, with 19 years to his credit. The short voyages to Portugal were sufficient inducement to stay on the old ship as long as possible.

My reason for being there was different: I didn't have much seatime left to do for a 2nd Mate's certificate, and that was the only vessel with guaranteed short enough voyages.

We loaded general cargo for Portugal and sailed from Glasgow on 1 February. During the war, ships' lifeboats were swung out before going to sea. Once again, a new engine in one of the boats added too much weight and pulled the davits out of the deck. The ship weighed anchor off Greenock and returned to Glasgow for repairs. Extensive alterations to all lifeboat davits were carried out and we didn't leave Glasgow until 3 March.

Everyone sailing on a merchant ship during the war signed on articles in some capacity. Civilian passengers weren't exempt, but were seldom carried. On that trip we had one passenger who was the wife of a manager with the Spanish Rio Tinto mines, in which the shipping company had an interest. She rejoined just before we sailed from Glasgow for the second time.

The cargo in the 'midship hold was mainly Scotch whisky, and this would be replaced for the return passage with large containers of port wine. To a Scot, it didn't seem a fair exchange, as whisky was strictly rationed in Glasgow and only American servicemen could afford to buy it on the black narket at £3 a bottle.

The other apprentice had been on the *Forbes* for more than two years, and the only ports he had been to were Glasgow, Lisbon and Huelva, with occasional calls at Gibraltar for convoy. He was a public

George Gunn in Lisbon, wearing a suit he had made himself.

Baron Forbes 1915-1963: built in Germany 1915 and surrendered to Great Britain as prize ship in 1919, operated by Hogarth 1922-1953, then scrapped.

schoolboy and a bit of an academic, with a hobby writing poetry. One of the sparks, a red-haired Irishman from Belfast, had been at sea for almost three years, but had never reached a foreign port. The three ships he had sailed on had all been sunk before he got anywhere. We couldn't understand why he still wanted to do it. On the last ship, his nerves had saved his life. He sat in the radio room wearing a lifejacket and with the door wide open. Immediately the torpedo struck, he ran across to the rail, jumped over the side and was picked up. He was the only survivor.

Because of the remote life they led, seamen were superstitious. Irish sparks was considered a bad omen. He was an easy-going person, and to be called a Jonah by some of the crew didn't bother him.

On the *Forbes*, the two apprentices ate in the dining saloon with the officers. I thought this was a real privilege and my first step up the ladder. The Irish sparks and the lady passenger were good bridge players but needed two more for a game. None of the other officers were interested, and we were told to try and learn how to play so that we could entertain the passenger. It was the best order we got that trip

and we worked hard at it. Unfortunately, the Atlantic weather intervened, and when the cards started to slide off the table the passenger retired and that was the end of the bridge.

The ship arrived Lisbon on 13 March and tied up at her usual general cargo berth, with easy access to the city centre. The whisky was unloaded first, under armed guard. We spoke about the shortages back home and came to the conclusion that the Portuguese were doing alright. Dave said, 'It's not all for Lisbon. Some of it goes to Germany.'

I asked Dave how he knew our Scotch whisky was going to Germany. On a number of occasions he saw it being loaded into rail cars marked Hamburg. 'And no doubt they're drinking our health with it now in Berchtesgarden and Berlin,' he said, rubbing it in.

Immediately the ship berthed, an official from the British Embassy boarded and gave the crew a talk on security precautions when ashore. Although they were not quite as numerous as they had been in the earlier years of the war, many enemy agents still worked in Lisbon and targeted British seamen. From time to time, some were identified and extradited to Germany. One ship's steward, whose vessel periodically called there,was sent back to the UK, tried for treason and executed.

On one of his first trips to Portugal my new colleague Dave met an English ex-pat in a cinema foyer and chatted about home. On the next visit he ran into him again, and was invited to an apartment for a drink. While there, he picked up a British newspaper, which was lying on top of a pile of magazines. Some of those at the bottom of the pile were in German. Dave reported it to the embassy, and the next time the Forbes called at Lisbon he was thanked and told that that particular agent was now back in Germany.

It was difficult to accept that Portugal, Britain's oldest ally, was harbouring Nazis. British Embassy officials had a real job on their hands.

During the war, Lisbon was one of the liveliest and most interesting ports ships visited. It was understandable why officers and crews wanted to stay on the *Forbes*.

Nineteen days in Lisbon discharging a nice clean general cargo was a sailor's dream. The ship had been on that run for so many years that everything was routine, even Sunday-afternoon football matches against local Portuguese teams at Estoril. The brightly-lit shops, full of everything unobtainable in war-torn Britain, were breathtaking. Unfortunately, after two weeks' shore expenses, there was nothing left from an apprentice's wages to buy luxury goods for home.

We left Lisbon on 5 April for Gibraltar, and joined a homeward-bound convoy for the UK. On some trips the ship sailed independently up the coast, then out into the Atlantic to join the convoy there. The coastal passage brought her well within range of enemy aircraft bases in France. Dave said it was safe enough as the Forbes was well known to the Germans, and they didn't intend to cut off their only guaranteed supply of Scotch. On a previous trip, heading up from Lisbon accompanied by another vessel, a German plane staying well out of range, flew overhead for a good look. It circled above the *Forbes*, turned round, went back, and attacked the other ship, then flew off in the direction of Finisterre, where it was shot down.

The main convoy broke up at Loch Ewe and a coastal one took over. We sailed round the north of Scotland and down to Leith for a few days, then on to the Tyne, where the articles were closed. After more than 20 years, the *Forbes* had made her last voyage between Glasgow and Lisbon.

New articles were opened on 3 May, at Mill Dam shipping office at South Shields. I was promoted to 3rd Mate and signed on 10 May 1944 for a trip to the West Indies via New York. For that ship and its regular crew, it really was a foreign voyage.

Captain Lachlan McPhail didn't like convoys, particularly steaming in one 3,000 miles across the Atlantic. The engineers and firemen had enough trouble raising sufficient steam to maintain station on short passages down to Gibraltar. By the time the ship got as far as Methil in Scotland, all five firemen had had enough, and Lachie had had enough of them. His log book entry read: 'this is to certify that the following members of the firemen are unable to carry out their duties as such, being utterly incompetent for maintaining steam and having no previous experience as firemen. James Hall - Anthony Crooks - Malachy Duggan - H. Meaney & E. Gorman. All procured from the Tyne Pool. It is necessary to procure proper firemen to enable steamer to continue on voyage.'

The cook lasted until Methil, when he was paid off sick. His replacement also had a certificate, but couldn't cook either, and left the ship in New York. After a couple of his breakfasts, I lost my taste for ship's porridge. The last straw came when I pulled what I thought was a hair out of my mouth and found it to be a cockroache's feeler. When I inspected the galley, it was easy to see where the cockroaches came from. The heat on the steel deckhead above the galley stove attracted them and they fell down into the large porridge pan simmering on top of the stove. I asked the cook if he ate porridge himself. He said he didn't like it. The currant buns he made as a special treat were so heavy, the seagulls in Loch Ewe couldn't lift them off the water.

The new firemen managed enough steam to get the ship into her convoy station, but maintaining it was a problem. Before the end of each watch, they pulled the fires, removed clinker, and banked them up ready for the next crowd coming on. That was the crucial time, the steam pressure went down and the ship dropped back. We got many encouraging messages on corvettes' loud hailers, such as, 'if you don't

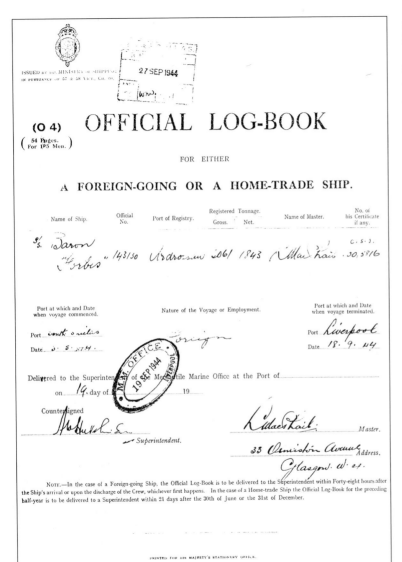

Baron Forbes log book.

get back into position we'll bloody well leave you behind'. It seemed inevitable.

My evening 8-12 watches in convoy were kept accompanied by the Old Man. As the ship dropped back, he coerced the engineers down the voice pipe to put her up two more revs. The order was acknowledged each time but the ship's speed never seemed to increase. He would hand me his pocket watch and say, 'Take this, stand over that engine room skylight and count them.' He would then shout down to the engineer, 'How many are you doing now?' Whatever the reply, Lachie's response was always, 'You're a bliddy liar. The 3rd Mate's just counted.'

The convoy disappeared in the distance and three days later we arrived in New York. The cook pleaded sickness and the Old Man was delighted to pay him off. He signed on a DBS who was ashore in New York because his own ship had been sunk. Getting paid for his passage back home instead of travelling as a Distressed British Seaman encouraged the new cook to produce the first decent meals we had had since leaving the Tyne.

Sailing independently was an opportunity to do some serious navigation as an officer of the watch. Lachie would take a cursory look at the chart from time to time to see where I had plotted the ship's position. Basic as they were, we navigated by instruments; he seemed to do it by instinct and used the stem of his pipe to measure distances. Pointing to his estimated position on a chart resulted in a series of tobacco stains right across the Atlantic Ocean.

After the ship left New York, I went on watch at 8 p.m. The south-bound convoy for the West Indies was forming. When I went below at midnight, we still hadn't managed to get on station, and at eight the following morning there wasn't another vessel in sight. Under these circumstances, merchant ships bound south were routed by the US Navy close inshore all the way down the coast. Ships were supplied with American charts drawn to a larger scale than Lachie had ever seen before. He was happy; the weather was fine and we had got rid of the convoy. Also, as the Old Man said, 'it is a more natural way to get around anyway.'

The ship anchored off Key West on Independence Day. It was a holiday and it was hot. We had sailed close inshore off Palm Beach,

Florida, surrounded by fine-looking pleasure cruisers and tuna fishing boats. Their colourfully painted superstructures, gleaming hulls and suntanned passengers contrasted vividly with a drab old, weatherbeaten tramp steamer which apparently had strayed well of its course. Palm Beach was the most beautiful place I had ever seen, and I decided there and then that I would go there some day when war was over. I went on a number of occasions, some 40 years later, and sat on an hotel balcony on the beach, looking out at similar scenes but under different circumstances.

The ship carried on to Georgetown, British Guyana, to load sugar for the UK. In 1944, it was a hot uncomfortable mosquito-infested place, and our initial instinct was to load the cargo and get away as soon as possible. When the ship berthed alongside, we found the residents, mainly British ex-pats, kind, fun-loving and very hospitable to ships' officers and crews.

While we were at anchor, a young naval officer boarded and I showed him to the Captain's cabin. Shortly, Lachie shouted 'Third. Mate, put this man back in his boat and don't allow him on board until he learns how to address people.' It turned out that he had called the captain 'skipper'. The Old Man had told him that this wasn't a fishing boat, and he was no skipper. With my help, he asked again for the 'Master' of the vessel. They parted good friends.

Bookers of Liverpool appeared to run everything in Georgetown. They had two vessels trading there regularly, and most of the British residents worked for the company. We were bound for Liverpool and it was probably Booker's sugar we loaded in Georgetown.

It was a change to stay up on deck when we loaded sugar in the West Indies. My promotion to 3rd Mate excused me from working long shifts down the holds with the dockers, and I was very happy to have a supervisory role, ensuring that the apprentices dunnaged as well as I had done it myself.

The ship only loaded part cargo and topped up in Port of Spain, Trinidad. We played a football match, against the Army, who turned out in their bare feet. Any advantage was lost as we couldn't catch them, and the exhausting heat did the rest. The match was followed by a Demerara special, a swizzle party given by the residents. They filled large punch bowls with rum and other liquid ingredients and everyone competed for the frothiest result with the adept use of a swizzle stick; then they drank it. The cargo was quickly loaded and it was on to Trinidad, then a convoy up to New York.

The ship berthed at a pier in the middle of Manhattan and stayed there for three weeks, waiting for a slow enough convoy back to the UK. Our reputation for losing convoys must have spread. There was no cargo loaded or unloaded, and with little else for the officers to do on board there was plenty time ashore.

Throughout our long stay, New York was at its sweltering worst. It was uncomfortable ashore during the day, and on board all the time. A shore doctor confirmed I had asthma and the only relief he recommended was an extra pillow from the Chief Steward.

The asthma disappeared as soon as the ship cleared the Hudson River and I never had it again. We tried to get our heads down during the day and went ashore, about ten at night, arriving back aboard at five in the morning. It was usually a midnight movie, Jack Dempsey's until four, spaghetti and meatballs for breakfast, then back to the ship.

Although the long stay in New York, with little to do on board, was unusual and enjoyable, it was a relief to get back to sea again. The D. Day Landings in Europe took place during our voyage to the West Indies. Having volunteered to go on one of the ships involved, and finding myself in the Caribbean instead, was quite a disappointment. We heard later that the *Forbes* was taken off the Lisbon run by the Ministry and sent for the sugar cargo to get her out of the way, thereby releasing a more suitable vessel for the landings. Nobody had the nerve to tell that to Lachie.

The slow convoy sailed from New York, and on this occasion we arrived at the destination with the other ships. Our method of keeping station was now tolerated by the escorts. Before steam started to drop, we pressed on until almost abeam of the ship ahead, and by the time we fell back on station the steam pressure was up on the mark again. Being allowed to behave like that in convoy gave the feeling the battle of the Atlantic was at last being won, although another 60 British merchant ships were sunk before it ended.

When the ship signed off on 19 August in Liverpool, I had enough seatime to study and sit for a 2nd Mate Certificate. Three and a half months as uncertificated 3rd Mate at £17.10/- a month, plus War Bonus and £50 accumulated Indenture Money, was sufficient to pay for a 3-month navigation course at Glasgow Royal Technical College, but I had to pass the exam first time.

I asked Lachie for a reference. He kindly said, 'You don't need a reference from me. You'll get on well enough in this business without it.' He did however relent and I left the ship with the reference and a belief I had chosen the right career after all.

Captain Lachlan McPhail and his *Baron Forbes* took part in a number of unusual incidents during the War. Knowingly or unknowingly helping to supply the German High Command with their favourite tipple was one, and, more significantly, another was enacted the previous year in Huelva.

S.S. "BARON FORBES."

LIVERPOOL.

H. HOGARTH & SONS,
GLASGOW.

19th SEPTEMBER 1944

To whom it may concern,

This is to certify that G.Gunn has served on the above named vessel under my command from January 10th 1944 to May 2nd 1944 as Apprentice,and from May 10th 1944 to September 18th 1944 as Third Officer.

During such times I found him an obedient and reliable seaman,and attentive to his duties as an Officer at all times. He now leaves to sit for an examination for Second Mate's Certificate in which I wish him every success.

Master.

Baron Forbes leaving certificate, 1944.

He was asked by Consular officials to attend the funeral of a British army officer, whose body was washed up near the port and brought ashore by Spanish fishermen. Lachie, being well known to the Spanish authorities, was an obvious choice to represent his country at the officer's funeral on foreign soil. He didn't know then, or even when I sailed with him, that he had played a part in one of the most important events which took place during the War.

The story is told in John Winton's essay, 'The War At Sea 1939-1945'; from Ewan Montagu's *The Man Who Never Was* (Hutchinson, 1967). Briefly, what happened was this. After the North African landings, the next obvious target was Sicily; so obvious that, as Churchill said, 'anybody but a damned fool would know it was Sicily'. However, in the Admiralty an ingenious plan, with the somewhat macabre code name 'Operation Mincemeat', was devised to hoodwink the German High Command that Sicily was only a cover target, the real objectives being Sardinia in the west and Greece in the east. The body of an unknown serviceman dressed as 'Major Martin', a Royal Marine officer on Mountbatten's staff, was dropped over the side from the submarine HMS/M *Seraph* off the south coast of Spain, in a position where it would surely drift inshore and come to the notice of the Spanish authorities. Major Martin's briefcase contained what purported to be vital secret documents outlining Allied plans for the future; among them a personal letter to General Alexander from General Archibald Nye (and actually written by him).

To make Major Martin 'real' he was provided with all his private impediments: identity card, passes, theatre ticket stubs, keys, money and personal letters, including two from his fictional fiancée.

After the war, captured German records showed that the German High Command swallowed 'Mincemeat' whole.

CHAPTER 10   The *Baron Douglas*: The End of the War at Sea

There were no correspondence courses or studying facilities on tramp steamers in the 1940s. When an apprentice or cadetship at sea ended, the majority went to technical college and started to learn navigation from scratch. Boys who left school at 14 or 15 years of age knew nothing about logarithms or spherical trigonometry or other basic principles of modern navigational practices. There was a lot of learning to do to reach the standard required for examination entry, and not much time in which to do it. A secondary school education was a good start, but all aspiring ships' officers didn't have that benefit. Failing a 2nd Mate's ticket meant a period back at sea or in many cases permanent employment as a deckhand in ships' forecastles with little chance of progression. There was every incentive to study hard. I passed the exam in December 1944 and joined the *Douglas* as 2nd Mate on 15 January 1945.

Looking for something different, I tried the officers' Pool in Glasgow and turned down the first three ships on offer. One was an old oil tanker, the second was two years on an RFA water boat based at Trincomalee in Ceylon, and the last was a vessel called Blairspey, well known to seamen as one to be avoided if possible.

Captain James Blackwood was master of the Douglas; he was also on the *Renfrew* when she was abandoned in the Atlantic. He instructed me to sign on a full crew at Mill Dam shipping office on Friday. He was going away for the weekend and wanted the ship ready to sail on Monday. I had never signed on a crew before, but he said, most of the work was done by the shipping master and that there would be no problems. He had already opened the articles himself. I managed to sign the officers, deck crew and stewards. All the firemen wanted large advances and allotments which their wages wouldn't cover, so they refused to sign and left the office.

The shipping master suggested that I went across to the union and had a word with them, as there was no chance of getting more firemen for Monday and the ship wouldn't sail. The captain would have been in real trouble, as he had gone to Hull on personal business and hadn't left her telephone number.

There was every reason to humour the firemen, and with humble pie if necessary. I told them the trouble I would have if they didn't join the ship; it was first job as 2nd Mate and probably my last. I went back to the shipping office and shortly after they all trooped in and signed. I hoped this was an example of what could be expected of Geordie firemen.

The ship left the Tyne as scheduled on 23 January, loaded a bulk cargo of pitch at Hull and sailed for the Med on 9 February. We called at Oran in North Africa, then on to Marseilles, picked up a pilot for Sete and docked there on the 27th.

It took some time to discharge the pitch as the water temperature caused it to melt a bit in the holds, and we were there for about ten days. This was enough time to see the mess the port was left in after the recent German occupation, and the bitter fighting which took place in that area before its recapture.

The port of Sete was under the control of a Royal Naval officer who advised ships' crews on procedures when ashore. The Old Man told me not to issue any money to the crew as it had no value. He suggested they would be better off drawing a couple of flat 50 tins of cigarettes from the steward, as that would pay for everything in any café in Sete. We tried it ourselves and it worked. One tin each bought an evening's supply of drinks and lots of attention from girls who vied with each other to try out their English. One said about another, 'she very bad girl. She go with *les Boches*.' I wondered what she herself had done during the four long years of German occupation. It looked like free haircuts all round once things settled down and recriminations started.

We left Sete and Marseilles in ballast on 10 March and anchored at Gibraltar for four days, before carrying on to the Gold Coast port of Takoradi to load a cargo of ore for the UK. In those days, Takoradi consisted of a few houses, a market place with smells and the end of a conveyor belt which delivered the ore to the ships from quarries miles away in the jungle.

We loaded in a couple of days, arrived at Freetown on 6 April, then we sailed on to Gibraltar and a convoy to London. The cargo was discharged at Greys in Essex and we departed from there on 6 May and arrived at the Tyne the following day.

Baron Douglas at Bona Vista Bay, loading for home after last convoy of the war, photographed by 2nd Mate (the author), 1945.

Baron Douglas aground (after post-war refit) – waiting to be refloated.

SCALE OF PROVISIONS

REQUIRED BY SECTION 25 OF THE MERCHANT SHIPPING ACT, 1906, AS AMENDED BY THE MERCHANT SHIPPING (SEAMEN'S PROVISIONS) ORDER, 1939, TO BE ALLOWED AND SERVED OUT TO THE CREW DURING THE VOYAGE, EXCEPT IN CASES IN WHICH THE CREW FURNISH THEIR OWN PROVISIONS.

Note.—The scale agreed upon is in addition to the Lime or Lemon Juice and Sugar, or other Anti-Scorbutics required by the Merchant Shipping Acts.

Article.	Allowance per week.	Article.	Allowance per week.
Water	28 quarts.	Milk { Condensed	9¼ ozs.
Soft Bread	7 lbs.	or	
Fresh Meat	8¼ lbs.	Dried	4 ozs.
Fresh Fish	*See note 1 below and paragraphs 3, 4 and 5 of Conditions and Exceptions.*	Milk for cooking { Condensed	4¼ ozs.
Eggs		or	
Smoked Ham or Bacon		Dried	2 ozs.
Potatoes	7 lbs.	Butter (see note 2 below)	¼ lb.
Dried or Compressed Vegetables	¼ lb.	Marmalade or Jam	¼ lb.
Peas, Split	½ lb.	Syrup	2 ozs.
Green Peas, Haricot Beans or Butter Beans	1¼ lbs.	Cheese	4 ozs.
Flour	2 lbs.	Suet	4 ozs.
Rice	6 ozs.	Pickles	¼ pint
Oatmeal, Rolled Oats or similar cereal	6 ozs.	Onions	¼ lb.
Tea	3 ozs.	Dried Fruits	5 ozs.
Coffee (containing not more than 25 per cent. Chicory)	2 ozs.	Fine Salt	2 ozs.
or		Mustard	¼ oz.
Cocoa (or Chocolate)	3 ozs.	Pepper	¼ oz.
Sugar (see note 2 below)	1¼ lbs.	Curry Powder	¼ oz.

NOTE 1.—The limitation on the use of fresh fish, eggs and smoked ham or bacon as equivalents for fresh meat means that the maximum amount which can be deducted from the weekly ration of fresh meat, in respect of these equivalents, is 2 lbs. 3 ozs.

NOTE 2.—The amounts of sugar and butter shown in the above scale are exclusive of the amounts used in the preparation of meals.

CONDITIONS AND EXCEPTIONS IN APPLYING SCALE.

1. GENERAL.—The issue of the provisions referred to in the above scale shall be reasonably distributed throughout the week ; and in the case of water, soft bread, meat and potatoes the issue shall be approximately equal each day.

2. BREAD.—The issue of soft bread under the scale shall not be required :—
  (a) in a ship of less than 1,000 tons gross registered tonnage ; or
  (b) if rough weather or illness, or absence of cook, or force majeure renders the making of bread impracticable ;
but where soft bread is not issued, an equivalent amount of biscuit stored in sealed tins shall be issued instead.

3. MEAT.—The term " Meat " includes " Pork ". The weight of fresh meat is the weight, including fat, and bone, before preparation for cooking.

When fresh meat is not available, salt or preserved meat may be substituted in the proportion of ⅔ lb. of salt meat or ½ lb. of preserved meat for 1 lb. of fresh meat.

Fresh offal and fresh sausage count as the equivalent of fresh meat. Other sausage counts as preserved meat.

Smoked ham or bacon should, when procurable at reasonable cost, be supplied to the extent of 6 ozs. weekly but not exceeding 8 ozs. and count as preserved meat.

NOTE.—In ships with no refrigerator it is undesirable that reliance should be placed on fresh meat keeping in good condition for more than 15 days from the date on which it is taken on board.

4. FISH.—The weight of fresh fish is the gross weight before preparation for cooking.

Fresh fish up to an amount not exceeding 1½ lbs. per week may be substituted for fresh meat and shall be regarded as equivalent to two-thirds of its weight of fresh meat.

In any week in which less than 8 ozs. of fresh fish is issued there shall be issued fish of a fatty type, such as kippers or tinned salmon, herrings, pilchards or sardines, the weight of which shall be one-half the amount by which the fresh fish issued is less than 8 ozs. Dried fish or tinned salmon, herrings, pilchards or sardines may be substituted for fresh fish in the proportion of 1½ ozs. of dried fish or 1 oz. of tinned fish to 2 ozs. of fresh fish.

5. EGGS.—Not less than four eggs, fresh or preserved in shell, shall be issued during the first fortnight of any voyage starting from a port within home trade limits, and two eggs for each week thereafter should be issued, if obtainable at a reasonable price, and if there are facilities for keeping them. Each egg so issued shall be regarded as the equivalent of 1½ ozs. of fresh meat under the scale. Eggs in excess of these may be issued, but shall not count against the scale.

6. POTATOES.—Fresh potatoes (when procurable in a sound condition) must be issued for at least the first eight weeks of the voyage in the case of every ship leaving a port within the home trade limits, at any time between the last day of September and the first day of May, and at any other time when they can be procured at a reasonable cost.

When fresh potatoes are not so issued, an equal amount of rice, yams, sweet potatoes, or vegetables preserved in tins, or an equivalent amount of dried or compressed potatoes or dried or compressed vegetables in the proportion of 1 lb. to 6 lbs. of fresh potatoes, or fresh bread in the proportion of 1 lb. of bread to 1 lb. of fresh potatoes, must be issued in their place.

7. DRIED MILK.—Dried milk may only be issued in lieu of condensed milk where the conditions on board are such as enable it to be kept in good condition in a cool, dry place, for the period during which it may be required.

8. VEGETABLES.—Fresh vegetables should be supplied as often as possible when they can be procured at a reasonable cost and are not likely to be injurious to health.

On each day when ½ lb. of fresh vegetables (or vegetables preserved in tins) is supplied, these are to be regarded for purposes of the scale as equivalent to one day's supply of dried or compressed vegetables and of green peas, haricot or butter beans.

9. DRIED FRUITS.—Dried fruits issued under the above scale must be raisins, sultanas, currants, figs, prunes, apples, pears, peaches or apricots.

10. ONIONS.—The onions to be issued under the above scale must be fresh, store or dried onions when in season ; and when fresh, store or dried onions are not in season, an equal amount of onions or other vegetables preserved in tins, or an equivalent amount of dried or compressed onions or other vegetables in the proportion of 1 oz. to ½ lb. of fresh onions must be issued.

11. The stokehold hands are to receive sufficient oatmeal and one quart of water extra daily while under steam.

NOTE.—In any case where tinned provisions are issued, the weight thereof shall be calculated exclusive of the container.

SUBSTITUTES AND EQUIVALENTS—NOT TO BE USED WITHOUT REASONABLE CAUSE.

Salt Meat	¾ lb.	To be considered equal to 1 lb. Fresh Meat.
Preserved Meat	½ lb.	
Coffee	1 oz.	To be considered equal.
Cocoa or Chocolate	1½ ozs.	
Tea	½ oz.	
Flour	1 lb.	To be considered equal.
Biscuit	1 lb.	
Rice	1 lb.	
Oatmeal, Rolled Oats or similar cereals ...	1 lb.	
Split Peas	½ lb.	To be considered equal when issued with meat rations.
Flour	¾ lb.	
Green Peas, Haricot or Butter Beans	½ lb.	
Rice	¾ lb.	

Marmalade	1 lb.	To be considered equal.
Jam	1 lb.	
Syrup	1 lb.	
Butter	½ lb.	
Cheese	½ lb.	
Condensed Milk	9½ ozs.	To be considered equal.
Dried Milk	4 ozs.	
Mustard		To be considered equal.
Curry Powder		

As the ship entered the Tyne at 5.00 p.m. on 7 May 1945, every vessel started blowing whistles, fog horns and anything else that would make a noise. It was the end of the war with Germany and a wonderful time to arrive at a home port.

I caught the train to Glasgow the following evening. The Central Station was a heaving mass of people of all ages, singing, dancing and celebrating. It was unforgettable.

The crew were paid off at South Shields; new articles opened immediately, and another crew signed on. We sailed one week later to join a Western Ocean convoy at Belfast Lough and left there on 22 May.

A few days out, a flag signal was hoisted from the Commodore ship, the gist of which read: 'This is your last North Atlantic convoy. All ships will disperse and proceed independently to the various destinations.' There was also a goodwill message from the Commodore, the text of which I can't recall. We arrived Bay Bulls in Newfoundland to discharge shale ballast loaded for the passage across from the UK, and from there went coastwise to load pulp wood at Indian Bay for Cornerbrook.

The ship anchored in Indian Bay and started loading on 12 June. The cargo was floated down from the logging camps and towed in the form of large rafts around the ship and loaded directly from the water into the holds.

Indian Bay, like other places in Newfoundland, was remote. It took nine days to load, and on Sunday we held an open day on the ship for local residents. They came out in boats, dressed for the occasion, and most of them had never been on or near a ship before. They didn't see many strangers and the only time we went ashore in one of the lifeboats, children ran into their homes when they saw us walking up the street. Before 1948, when Newfoundland voted to enter the Canadian Federation, people in remote areas existed in another age. They lived mainly off fish, and when I asked about meat one said: 'Eli killed a moose last year'.

We sailed from Indian Bay on 21 June, fully loaded, and with a 15-foot-high deck cargo, and arrived at Cornerbrook on the 24th and left on the 27th.

Many of the crew were still ashore at sailing time. There seemed to be very few men in Cornerbrook, but lots of girls; many of whom came there from outside the town to work at Bowater's paper factory. They didn't meet a lot of strangers and made members of our crew most welcome.

Blackwood told me to get a cab and round up the crew. I managed to put them all on board; some were logged as deserters, others as being unfit for duty. They were all fined. This ship started from the UK with crew problems, which continued throughout the voyage. So much for white crews.

Our next stop was Dingwall, Novas Scotia, to load gypsum for New York. The ship arrived on 28 June and sailed on the 30th. The only Dingwall I had been to before was in the north of Scotland. There wasn't much difference between them. They were both populated by Scots, but in Nova Scotia they seemed even more patriotic than those in Ross-shire. Being a Scottish registered ship, the officers were invited to a ceilidh ashore. There, the residents wore kilts, played bagpipes, and probably reminisced about the Old Country, and asked themselves why they ever came to live in such a God-forsaken place. Loading gypsum in Dingwall was a continual, steady process so nobody on the ship could accept the invitation. There was only one berth and one pilot and ships strictly took it in turn to load. For as long as the gypsum trade lasted in Dingwall, the same pilot docked, shifted, and sailed every vessel himself. Forty years after, I called when touring in Nova Scotia and he was still living there. He saw the end of the gypsum, but it never saw the end of him.

On the way down to New York, we stopped at Sydney, Cape Breton, to put a sailor ashore, whose finger I unsuccessfully lanced a couple of weeks previously in Indian Bay. We left Sydney the following day and reached Brooklyn on 5 July. It took just two days to discharge and we managed a night ashore in Manhattan. I bought a guitar in a second-hand shop off Broadway and left it at a check-in in Times Square subway. Outside there, we were coaxed into a DIY recording kiosk and I made a record of 'When Day Is Done'. Ralph, our Canadian sparks, said he couldn't sing and would I do one for his wife in Saskatoon, Saskatchewan. I did 'Melancholy Baby'. We didn't realise that, as the recordings were being made, they were broadcast to passers-by on Broadway, who made their feelings known when we stepped out of the kiosk with the records.

More crew members' names were put in the official log book in New York for desertion, absence without leave and refusal to work; and the troubles looked like continuing until the ship got home.

We left New York for Newport News, Virginia and loaded coal for Newfoundland. The ship moored in St. John's and, day and night, other vessels tied up alongside to bunker. The coal lasted 12 days and we weren't sorry to see it go. After St. John's, it was up to another outpost, Bona Vista Bay, to load pit props for the UK. There was nowhere to go ashore there, and our off-duty periods were spent fishing and playing cards. Jigging with cod-hooks from a lifeboat brought in sufficient fish for all hands to have fresh cod steaks every day. This helped the cook and steward, as fresh food was even shorter than usual when anchored up the creeks and backwaters of Newfoundland. Most of the chief steward's career had been spent sailing between north-east England ports and the Baltic. One qualification must have been frugality, as he was really mean. A deckhand interrupted a game of pontoon in the dining saloon to tell him there was a shortage in their weekly food ration. The steward went into his cabin and gave the man a piece of cheese from under the pillow. During the war many ships' officers slept on their settees instead of the bunks. We hoped that this steward was one of them.

We arrived in St. John's on 12 August, loaded and with a 15-foot-high deck cargo of pit props, and left there for the UK after a very boisterous night ashore celebrating VJ Day on the 15th. The visibility leaving St. John's was poor, and we carried this all the way across the Atlantic before docking in Hull on 26 August. The war at sea was over at last, and I paid off this ship and went home to Glasgow to get married.

The author with his future wife.

Acknowledgement

For help in obtaining material for the compilation of the book I am indebted to:

THE WORLD SHIP SOCIETY – for access to their publication of *Hogarth History & Fleet List* by Leonard Gray and to my former Baron Line colleague A.A. McAlister.

THE REGISTRY OF SHIPPING & SEAMEN, Cardiff and STEPHEN NORRIS – former Transport Minister, for Log Book access.

THE MITCHELL LIBRARY, Glasgow and the staff for the facilities they provided and access to G. Langmuir shipping archive.

THE NATIONAL MARITIME MUSEUM, London, and THE IMPERIAL WAR MUSEUM, London, for convoy photographs.

ROD DYMOTT, of Cassells, for excerpts from *Experiences of War: The British Sailor* by Kenneth Poolman.
MICHAEL MONTGOMERY, author of *Who Sank the Sydney?*

SKYFOTOS – for copies of photographs of Baron Line ships.

COMMODORE CHARLES COLBURN, Swansea, former Senior Master B.P. Tanker Fleet, for his personal interest and advice.

ALAN BRADLEY, whose maps appear on p. 22 and p. 36.

MAIRWEN PRYS JONES at Gomer Press for 'Putting the Ship back on Course' from time to time.

Appendix 1: Estimated steaming distances in nautical miles

Voyage No. 19 – Trip No. 1
23 July 1941 / 24 February 1942
      Steaming distance   29, 400 miles
      Distance in convoy   9,500 miles
      Distance independently   19,900 miles

Voyage No. 20 – Trip No. 2
12 March 1942 / 24 February 1943
      Steaming distance   47,360 miles
      Distance in convoy   13,000 miles
      Distance independently   34,360 miles

Voyage No. 21 – Trip No. 3
3 March 1943 / 28 July 1943
      Steaming distance   12,500 miles
      Distance in convoy   10,500 miles
      Distance independently   2.000 miles

Voyage No. 22 – Trip No. 4
20 August 1943 / 27 November 1943
      Steaming distance   6,610 miles
      Distance in convoy   4,300 miles
      Distance independently   2,310 miles

Voyage No. 23 – Trip No. 5
3 March 1944 / 1 May 1944
      Steaming distance   4,450 miles
      Distance in convoy   4,000 miles
      Distance independently   450 miles

Voyage No. 24 – Trip No. 6
10 May 1944 / 18 September 1944
      Steaming distance   14,350 miles
      Distance in convoy   9,750 miles
      Distance independently   4,600 miles

Voyage No. 25 – Trip No. 7
23 January 1945 / 7 May 1945
      Steaming distance   11,780 miles
      Distance in convoy   4,400 miles
      Distance independently   7,380 miles

Voyage No. 26 – Trip No. 8
8 May 1945 / 28 August 1945
      Steaming distance   11,000 miles
      Distance in convoy   3,000 miles
      Distance independently   8,000 miles

Estimated total steaming distance from 23 July 1941 until 28 August 1845 – 137,450 nautical miles of which 58,450 were in North Atlantic and UK Coastal Convoys and 79,000 on Independently Routed Worldwide Trading.

Baron Renfrew, voyage Nos. 19 – 20 – 21
Baron Yarborough, voyage No. 48
Baron Forbes, voyage Nos. 177 – 178
Baron Douglas, voyage Nos. 35 – 36

Appendix 2: Hogarth steamers lost during World War II

Baron Ogilvy　　　　1926-1942　　　　Torpedoed by U-125 South West of Cape Palmas. Eight crew lost. Seen here loading general cargo with two other vessels at coal hoists.

Baron Newlands　　　　1928-1942　　　　Torpedoed by U-68 off Ivory Coast. Eighteen crew lost.

Baron Saltoun 1927-1940. Mined off Cherbourg.

Baron Kelvin	1924-1941	Torpedoed by U-206 14 miles off Spain.
Baron Erskine	1930-1942	Sunk by U-701 in North Atlantic. Captain and 39 crew lost.
Baron Ailsa	1936-1940	Struck mine NW of Cromer. Captain and one crew member lost.
Baron Jedburgh	1936-1945	Torpedoed by U-532 off Brazil. All but one of the crew saved.
Baron Minto	1937-1940	Wrecked when damaged by air attack off Rattray Head. Declared total loss.
Baron Semple	1939-1943	Sunk by U-848 NW off Ascension Island. Captain and all 62 crew members lost.

Baron Nairn	1925-1941	Torpedoed by U-108 west of Cape Race.
Baron Carnegie	1925-1941	Torpedoed by aircraft off St. David's Head. 25 crew lost.
Baron Lovat	1926-1941	Torpedoed by Italian submarine SW of Cape St. Vincent.
Baron Kinnaird	1927-1942	Torpedoed by U-653 in North Atlantic. Captain and all 40 crew lost.
Baron Elibank (II)	1923-1934	Torpedoed and sunk by U-37 about 250 miles off Lisbon. 7 of her crew were lost.
Baron Pentland	1927-1941	Torpedoed by U-652 off Cape Farewell then sunk by U372. 2 crew lost.
Baron Cochrane	1927-1942	Torpedoed by U-123 North of Azores. 2 crew lost.
Baron Loudon	1925-1940	Torpedoed by U-48 NW of Cape Ortegal, Brazil. 3 crew lost.
Baron Dechmont	1929-1943	Torpedoed by U-507 NW of Brazil. 7 crew lost, Captain taken prisoner on sub., then killed when it was bombed and sunk 10 days later.
Baron Blythswood	1929-1940	Torpedoed by U-99 South of Iceland. Captain and 33 crew lost.
Baron Jedburgh (II)		Torpedoed and sunk by U-532 NE of Bahia: all but one of the crew saved. The captain's boat reached the Brazilian coast 2 weeks afterwards.

Appendix 3: Ships managed by Hogarth lost in World War II

Ocean Vanquisher	1942	Sunk by Italian frogmen from the Submarine *Ambra* using a limpet mine N.W. of Algiers.
Empire Conveyor	1939-1940	Torpedoed by U-122 about 50 miles South of Barra Head. Captain killed.
Empire Progress	1940-1942	Bombed by aircraft then torpedoed and sunk by U-402. 11 crew lost.
Tysa	1940-1942	Torpedoed by Italian submarine in Atlantic then sunk by escort gunfire.
Yselhaven	1940-1942	Torpedoed by U-43 in North Atlantic. 24 crew lost.
Haulerwijk	1940-1941	Torpedoed by U-32 in North Atlantic 1200 miles West of Ireland.
Anadyr	1940-1944	Torpedoed by U-129 about 600 miles SE of Recife, Brazil.
Western Chief	1940-1941	Torpedoed by Italian submarine *Emo* 600 miles South of Iceland. 24 crew lost.
Ombilin	1942	Torpedoed by Italian submarine *Enrico Tazzoli* NW of Cesra, Brazil.
Ocean Voyager	1942-1943	Bombed and sunk in Tripoli Harbour. Captain and 4 crew killed, 10 wounded.
Fort Chilcotin	1942-1943	Torpedoed by U-172 about 750 miles Sth. of Recife, Brazil. 4 crew lost.

Appendix 4: Hogarth steamers lost in World War I

Baron Ogilvy (I)	1909-1917	Torpedoed and sunk by submarine 172 miles NW from Tory Island. Two of her crew were lost.
Baron Balfour	1901-1917	Torpedoed by U-46 8 miles North of Sein Island.
Baron Kelvin (I)	1903-1913	Sunk by gunfire from U-28, 95 miles West of Bishop Rock.
Baron Cawdor (II)	1905-1917	Torpedoed by U-26, 150 miles SW of Fastnet. 3 crew lost.
Baron Garioch (I)	1908-1917	Torpedoed by submarine 5 miles SE of Anvil Point. 2 crew lost.
Baron Napier (I)	1909-1926	Sold to the Japanese in 1926. Sunk by US submarine in 1944.
Baron Sempill (I)	1911-1917	Captured by U-44, 180 miles SW of Fastnet and sunk by bombs.
Baron Herries (I)	1907-1918	Torpedoed and sunk by U-91 43 miles from Bishop Rock. Three of her crew were lost.
Baron Erskine (I)	1911-1915	Torpedoed by U-38, 25 miles NNW of Bishop Rock.
Baron Tweedmouth (I)	1912-1916	Sunk by gunfire from U-34, 25 miles off Algeria.
Baron Ailsa (I)	1912-1918	Torpedoed by sub. 18 miles off Pembrokeshire; 10 crew lost.
Baron Wemyss (I)	1912-1917	Torpedoed by sub. 73 miles from Fastnet. 2 crew lost.
Baron Yarborough (I)	1913-1916	Captured by U-34 off Majorca and sunk by bombs.
Baron Blantyre (I)	1913-1917	Torpedoed by sub. 60 miles off Finisterre. 1 crew lost.
Saint Cecilia	1916	Mined 4 miles off Folkestone. Mine laid by German sub. UC8.
Baron Inchcape (I)	1916	Sold to Japan, torpedoed by US sub. *Thresher* in 1943.

Appendix 5: British Merchant Ship losses 1939-45

Year	Month	Ships	GRT*	Year	Month	Ships	GRT*	Year	Month	Ships	GRT*
1939	September	30	153,634		August	26	96,196		July	30	187,759
	October	21	104,712		September	57	214,664		August	14	62,900
	November	22	57,173		October	32	151,777		September	11	60.323
	December	23	103,496		November	26	90,711		October	11	57,565
					December	120	270,873		November	15	61,593
1940	January	24	101,869						December	10	55,611
	February	21	110,372	1942	January	27	147,716				
	March	13	39,302		February	59	314,029	1944	January	13	66,588
	April	9	74,838		March	67	250,679		February	11	63,180
	May	31	82,429		April	52	292,882		March	10	49,637
	June	61	282,560		May	56	258,245		April	3	21,439
	July	64	271,056		June	48	233,492		May	5	27,297
	August	56	278,323		July	41	232,454		June	16	54,611
	September	62	324,030		August	56	344,311		July	9	40,167
	October	63	301,892		September	50	274,952		August	17	80,590
	November	73	303,682		October	59	404,406		September	4	26,407
	December	61	265,314		November	76	474,606		October	1	1,155
					December	45	232,152		November	4	11,254
1941	January	41	208,567						December	10	46,715
	February	75	315,304	1943	January	18	91,056				
	March	83	364,575		February	29	166,247	1945	January	9	45,691
	April	75	361,578		March	61	384,898		February	12	43,449
	May	92	386,953		April	32	194,247		March	12	45,862
	June	60	268,548		May	31	146,496		April	9	52,131
	July	30	94,310		June	11	44,826		May	1	2,878

Total No. of Ships = 2,426
Gross Reg. Tonnage = 11,331,933

*Gross Registered Tonnage

By the same author:

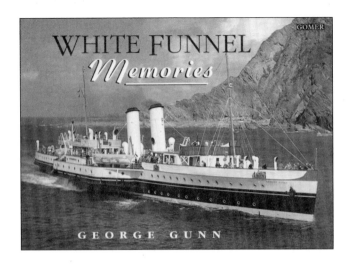

'Captain George Gunn was fortunate enough to command all the post-war White Funnel paddler steamers at one time or another. In this book, he describes his own experiences, together with anecdotes of the other characters who served the White Funnel company and its ships in the 50s and 60s. The Captains, Guv'nors, Pursers, and Engineers are all featured along with the ships themselves and the places they visited. Each chapter is accompanied by well chosen, high quality, photographs. My own favourites cover the grounding of Glen Usk on the Horseshoe bend in the River Avon. The photograph of the officers in conference is a classic, but there are many others to savour, and the front cover colour shot of Cardiff Queen entering Ilfracombe is truly wonderful.'

Paddle Wheels

'It is the 'warts and all' narrative of the last days of the paddle era which really excites the imagination. The author's splendid anecdotes, even those against himself, are recounted with the disarming Scottish wit of a born raconteur who loves his ships and likes people.'

Ships Monthly

'With about sixty photographs, this delightful book will appeal to anyone with even a remote interest in paddle steamers.'

Sea Breezes

'For thousands of us, trips to Ilfracombe or around the Gower coast are remembered as magical. Reading of the ships, their captains, crews, characters and ports of call, it is like a breath of fresh sea air.'

South Wales Evening Post

White Funnel Memories: George Gunn   ISBN 1 85902 487 4   £9.95